A-LEVEL YEAR 2

STUDENT GUIDE

EDEXCEL

Economics A

Theme 3

Business behaviour and the labour market

Marwan Mikdadi

PHILIP ALLAN FOR
HODDER
EDUCATION
AN HACHETTE UK COMPANY

Philip Allan, an imprint of Hodder Education, an Hachette UK company, Blenheim Court, George Street, Banbury, Oxfordshire OX16 5BH

Orders

Bookpoint Ltd, 130 Park Drive, Milton Park, Abingdon, Oxfordshire OX14 4SB

tel: 01235 827827

fax: 01235 400401

e-mail: education@bookpoint.co.uk

Lines are open 9.00 a.m.–5.00 p.m., Monday to Saturday, with a 24-hour message answering service. You can also order through the Hodder Education website: www.hoddereducation.co.uk

© Marwan Mikdadi and Rachel Cole 2016

ISBN 978-1-4718-5685-3

First printed 2016

Impression number 5 4 3 2 1

Year 2020 2019 2018 2017 2016

This Guide has been written specifically to support students preparing for the Edexcel A-level Economics A examinations. The content has been neither approved nor endorsed by Edexcel and remains the sole responsibility of the authors.

Typeset by Integra Software Services Pvt. Ltd., Pondicherry, India

Cover photo: ortodoxfoto/Fotolia

Printed in Italy

Hachette UK's policy is to use papers that are natural, renewable and recyclable products and made from wood grown in sustainable forests. The logging and manufacturing processes are expected to conform to the environmental regulations of the country of origin.

Contents

Content Guidance

Questions & Answers

■ Getting the most from this book

Exam tips

Advice on key points in the text to help you learn and recall content, avoid pitfalls, and polish your exam technique in order to boost your grade.

Knowledge check

Rapid-fire questions throughout the Content Guidance section to check your understanding.

Knowledge check answers

1 Turn to the back of the book for the Knowledge check answers.

Summaries

■ Each core topic is rounded off by a bullet-list summary for quick-check reference of what you need to know.

Exam-style questions

Commentary on the questions

Tips on what you need to do to gain full marks, indicated by the icon **e**

Questions & Answers

(b) Assess ways in which the Poundland and 99p Stores merger represents a principal–agent problem. *(10 marks)*

e A new kind of question based on a new element of the specification, and one in which candidates will struggle to relate textbook learning to the context.

(c) Apart from integration, discuss one non-pricing strategy that national discount retail chains might use to prevent further losses. Use game theory to support your answer. *(12 marks)*

e Game theory is used to model the behaviour of interdependent agents. It can take many forms. You might want to use a payoff matrix or Sweezy's kinked demand curve. There are several other valid approaches, too.

(d) Discuss the potential benefits of horizontal integration of firms in a market where profit margins are falling. *(8 marks)*

e This is a standard question on integration (most people will refer to economies of scale and increased market share) but with a twist – it must be related to falling profit margins.

(e) National discount retail chains such as Poundland and 99p Stores were investigated by the Competition and Markets Authority (CMA) in 2015 before the merger was allowed to take place. Discuss possible issues the CMA might face when attempting to regulate this industry. *(15 marks)*

e Remember that for this question you must make at least three if not four good solid points. It is a contextual question and you should show your understanding that market conditions have noticeably changed since the start of the credit crunch in 2007 when, in the UK, many firms went out of business. The context is important for this question.

Student answer

(a) The market structure of the national discount retail chains is an oligopoly. An oligopoly is a market where there are many firms, with three to eight firms dominating the market. There are high barriers to entry and exit, and firms supply similar products. Firms like Poundland, 99p Stores and Costcutters dominate the industry.

e 2/5 marks awarded. The student earns 1 mark for correctly identifying oligopoly, but the explanation is not entirely convincing. There are unlikely to be many firms, if there are just three to eight firms! A better approach would be to say 'a few firms dominate the market'. Another approach is to use the rule of thumb that 'five or fewer firms control at least 50% of the market'.

The application marks are 1 out of 2 marks. The application simply lists the national discount retail chains, it does not actually identify any of the barriers to entry or exit, such as strong brand loyalty in the national discount retail chains.

Sample student answers

Practise the questions, then look at the student answers that follow.

Commentary on sample student answers

Find out how many marks each answer would be awarded in the exam and then read the comments (preceded by the icon **e**) following each student answer. Annotations that link back to points made in the student answers show exactly how and where marks are gained or lost.

■ About this book

This book covers Theme 3 Business behaviour and the labour market of Edexcel's Economics A A-level. It gives an overview of the knowledge and skills required to achieve a high grade for questions in the Paper 1 and Paper 3 examinations. The aim of Theme 3 is to consider the role that firms play in the economy, their size, how they behave and what actions the government may take to regulate them.

Theme 3 is based on the theory of the firm and labour market, considering costs and revenues, market structures and the way in which firms behave, as well as behaviour of factor markets, in particular labour. It is based on principles such as the law of diminishing returns and the principles that govern demand, which are used to derive diagrams for both the short run, when at least one factor is fixed, and the long run, when all factors are variable.

The theoretical content has been divided into six main topics:

(1) Business growth. We look at reasons why firms may want to grow and how they grow. We consider the advantages of growth, why some very successful firms remain small, and why firms break up into smaller parts.

(2) Revenue, costs and profits. Using the concepts of the law of diminishing marginal productivity and economies of scale, we can derive the short- and long-run cost curves. Using price elasticity of demand, we can derive revenue and profit relationships.

(3) Business objectives. Initially we assume all firms aim to maximise profits and we use a simple formula to illustrate this: $MC = MR$. But profit maximisation brings with it dangers of new competitors or attracts the attention of the competition authorities. It is also a position that considers only short-term conditions, and it might be better to increase output or market share to guarantee long-run profits.

(4) Market structures. We consider the nature of competition in the market — how many buyers and sellers there are, the degree of market power each firm has, and how this affects efficiency. The extremes of competition range from perfect competition to monopoly. We also look at market power from the point of view of the buyer rather than that of the seller, a theory called **monopsony**. We look at contestability to see how easy it is for firms to enter and leave a market.

(5) Labour market. We look at the demand and supply of labour and the impact on the wage rate. This includes the demand for labour as a derived demand for a good or service. We look at problems which the government attempts to deal with in the labour markets, from wages that are too low or too high in free markets, to the policies governments may use to combat labour market immobility.

(6) Government intervention to maintain competition in markets. We consider why and how the government intervenes in markets, and how successful the government is in trying to regulate the behaviour of markets where markets on their own fail to produce optimum outcomes.

Content Guidance

■ Business growth

Sizes and types of firms

A **firm** is a production unit. It transforms resources into goods and services. 'Industry' is the term used to describe a collection of firms operating in the same production process. Firms aim to make profit and if they do not, they go out of business (unless they are state supported or have some other form of finance). If firms aim to make profit and can make more profit by growing, then firms will tend to grow.

Reasons why some firms tend to grow

Firms grow for a variety of reasons. They may decide to grow larger to:

- **increase market share** and hopefully become the dominant firm in a particular industry. This may allow them to increase their profits or ensure that they are in a stronger position to dominate the market, or set prices to their benefit.
- **benefit from greater profits.** A firm aims to maximise profits and may be able to achieve this through expansion, by increasing its sales, setting price or benefiting from lower costs of production.
- **increase sales**, through larger brand recognition and more sales outlets. These could be in the same country or even allow a firm to gain a presence abroad very quickly, with an already established brand name.
- **increase economies of scale.** The firm is able to exploit its increased size and to lower long-run average cost ($LRAC$). Furthermore, by driving down $LRAC$ and approaching the minimum point on the $LRAC$ curve, the firm is moving closer to productive efficiency.
- **gain power** so as to prevent potential takeovers by larger predator businesses, also allowing them to survive any major downturn in economic performance. For example, during the recession of 2009, a number of firms merged to ensure their long-term survival despite falling sales.
- **satisfy managerial ambitions.** Some managers will seek to grow their business so that they can satisfy their desire to run a successful business, see share prices rise if they receive shares as part of their remuneration, or leave a legacy of growth and acquisition after they have left.
- **make the most of an opportunity.** Some firms will have revenues that they do not want to class as 'profit' (subject to corporation tax) and so will use them to acquire another business.
- **gain expertise.** Some firms may wish to develop a new part of their business and rather than trying to establish themselves slowly, feel they can buy an existing market leader and with it its experience in the market.

Knowledge check 1

What is a firm?

Knowledge check 2

What is the difference between a firm and an industry?

Exam tip

Look in the business section of any quality newspaper and find an example of a growing firm. Ask yourself whether any of the reasons given here explain why the firm has grown large. Be prepared to repeat this process in an exam.

Reasons why some firms tend to remain small

While there are clear advantages to be gained from growth, it is obvious that some firms remain small for a number of reasons. See the section 'Constraints on business growth' (pages 9–12).

Significance of the divorce of ownership from control: the principal–agent problem

In cases where there are a large number of shareholders, the day-to-day management of the business is delegated to a board of directors and from them to their managers. In such cases there can be problems associated with divorce of ownership, known as the principal–agent problem. The principal is the shareholder or owner of a business, while the person in charge of the day-to-day running of the business is referred to as the agent. In such cases the agent can make decisions on behalf of the business that do not necessarily match the direction in which the owners would like to take the business. This can be a problem if the principal is not fully aware of the actions of the agent, as is often the case with large corporations, or they lack sufficient information, as a result of asymmetric information, covered in Theme 1. In such instances the manager (or agent) can behave in a way that conflicts with the objectives of the owners. This may result in the agent being dismissed when this comes to light. High-profile dismissals include that of Antony Jenkins of Barclays Bank in July 2015, who was said to have lost his job because, among other things, he was not able or willing to cut costs and therefore not able to increase profits fast enough.

Types of firm

Private sector

Private-sector firms are those that are not owned by the government. They may be owned by shareholders, as with a PLC (public limited company) such as Marks & Spencer, which is trading on a stock market and allows anyone to buy shares in it. Or they may be family owned, where the shares are not traded on the stock market, an example of which is LEGO, owned by the Christiansen family from Denmark.

Private-sector firms also include sole proprietors, which are owned and run by one person, such as a newsagent. Accountancy and legal firms form partnerships, which are owned by the partners.

Private-sector firms will aim to make a profit to satisfy the demands of their owners.

Public sector

The government may own certain businesses, either because they could not survive without significant state funding or because the government wishes to determine the direction the business takes. Examples of such businesses in the United Kingdom include the National Health Service, which relies on taxpayer funding, and Network Rail, which operates the UK's railway tracks but is owned by the government and run on the basis that it will not make a profit for shareholders but instead will reinvest any surplus funds.

Knowledge check 3

Is a large firm one that makes a high level of profit, one that makes a high level of sales or one that has a large number of employees?

Not for profit

The not-for-profit sector consists of charities, sometimes known as the third sector or civil society, which exist to provide services to local, national and international communities, and do not see profit as the primary goal. These include well-known charities such as Oxfam and less well-known organisations which act as local pressure groups or help in their local communities.

Business growth

How businesses grow

Organic growth

Firms can grow by expanding the scale of their operations and gaining market share. This is known as internal or **organic** growth and is achieved by investment within the firm by the firm. It is paid for either by ploughing back profits within the firm or by borrowing (loans or issuing more shares).

Advantages and disadvantages of organic growth

Organic growth tends to be the lowest-risk form of growth and the control of the firm remains unchanged. It means firms can build on existing strengths and continue to meet consumer expectations. Organic growth can also be good for the workers' morale and means there will be more job opportunities within the firm, with increased scope for management roles.

Disadvantages are that organic growth tends to be slow and building on the existing knowledge of existing workers means that people might be unaware of new ideas or innovations or unwilling to take on new ideas if they involve change.

Inorganic growth — integration of firms

Firms can also grow through takeovers (inorganic growth), of which there are a number of different types.

Horizontal integration

This is a merger between two firms at the same stage of production, for example the banks TSB and Banco Sabadell in June 2015 or the proposed merger of mobile phone operators O2 and 3 in March 2015. This kind of integration is often chosen to achieve economies of scale or to increase market share.

The advantages and disadvantages of **horizontal integration** are shown in Table 1 on page 10.

Vertical integration

This is a merger between firms at different stages of the productive process within an industry. The reason for this kind of integration is to increase **barriers to entry**, to increase control over suppliers or markets, or to ensure a smooth production process.

This can be further classified as:

- **Forward vertical integration**: at the next stage of the production process, e.g. American Apparel, which designs, manufactures and sells its products, buying design, manufacture and retail components.

Exam tip

The phrase 'we've always done it like this' is one of the key limitations to organic change. Organic growth requires the firm to overcome any inertia or resistance to change within the firm.

Exam tip

Internal growth is when a firm grows by investing in its current operations, or by extending its range of operations. External growth (or inorganic growth) is when a firm grows by joining with other firms, usually through a merger or takeover.

Horizontal integration Merger of two firms at the same stage of production.

Barriers to entry Obstacles to companies entering a market/ industry. These can be legal barriers imposed by government in the form of permits or patents required before a firm may participate in an industry, or they may be created by the firm in the form of advertising, brand loyalty or technical expertise.

Forward Merger with a firm at the next stage of production.

- **Backward vertical integration**: at the previous stage of the production process, e.g. RIL, an Indian petrol producer, buying an oil-extraction firm.

Advantages and disadvantages of vertical integration are shown in Table 1 on page 10.

Conglomerate integration

This is a merger between firms in entirely unrelated industries. The aim is often to achieve a greater spread of risk, widening the range of output to reduce exposure to any one market. It allows firms to use funds to cross-subsidise investment in new areas, taking the chance to innovate without losing their revenue drivers. A pioneer of conglomerate integration in the UK has been Richard Branson at Virgin, renowned for diverse investment and entrepreneurship.

Advantages and disadvantages of **conglomerate integration** are shown in Table 1 on page 10.

Constraints on business growth

Barriers to entry into or exit from an industry are obstacles that ensure the continued monopoly power of firms in a market.

Regulation

The government itself may prevent the entry or growth of a firm. Acts of parliament can allow monopolies to be formed and protected, such as the provision of the National Lottery. The former nationalised utilities, such as water, rail and electricity, were monopolies formed and protected by acts of parliament. **Patents** will also give firms legal protection to ensure that ideas or processes are protected from competition for the life of the patent. This is important in pharmaceuticals and high-tech industries where considerable money is invested in research and development, which will only be rewarded over time. Other industries require **licences** or specific qualifications before a firm or individual can operate. For example, law and accountancy firms have to be approved by their respective trade bodies, and radio stations have to obtain a licence before they can broadcast.

Marketing barriers

Marketing barriers are those imposed by businesses currently operating in an industry. This could be through branding or a new advertising campaign to re-establish brand recognition. The investment in marketing cannot be recouped if the campaign fails – this is known as **sunk costs**. For example, Coca-Cola spent millions in trying to bring its purified tap water Dasani to the UK market, but the product failed to take off after negative publicity. Most companies do not have the capacity to take such a risk.

Pricing barriers

Firms already in the market may try to prevent new firms entering in two very distinct ways. See the section on pricing strategies on page 23.

Technical barriers

Often, a few large firms dominate an industry thanks to their size. They use existing technical expertise and economies of scale to ensure that they operate at the lowest possible average cost, and new firms entering the industry will find it impossible to

Backward Merger with a firm at the previous stage of production.

Conglomerate merger Merger between firms in unrelated industries.

Knowledge check 4

A train-operating company buys a media firm. What kind of integration is this?

Exam tip

When asked about types of integration, note that on a 4-mark question, 2 of the marks will be assigned to application. Use the context provided for the firms involved to explain the answer.

Exam tip

A contestable market is one that has low or no barriers to entry or exit. Markets that are not contestable will have high sunk costs such as advertising, the cost of which a firm may not recover once it has been spent.

Type of merger	Definition	Recent example	Advantage to firms	Disadvantage to firms	Advantage to employees or other stakeholders	Disadvantage to employees or other stakeholders
Horizontal merger	Firms joining at the same stage of the production process	In June 2015 TSB Bank merged with Sabadell Bank of Spain	Increased market share; economies of scale; reduced competition	Risks – 'too many eggs in one basket'; unknown costs; weakening or 'dilution' of brand	Some opportunities for promotion; increased prestige of firm	Loss of jobs for those duplicating work or unable to move to new headquarters
Horizontal demerger	Firms splitting at the same point of the production process	BHP Billiton, a mining company, sold off South 32 in May 2015 to allow it to concentrate on core products such as iron ore, coal and copper, with South 32 specialising in aluminium, silver and nickel	Reduced exposure to what might be a risky market; removal of diseconomies of scale	Might be seen as a sign of weakness; share price might fall	Less risk in the company might mean increased job security	Some loss of jobs as parts of the business are pared down
Backward vertical merger	A firm merges with a firm closer to the suppliers in a production process	Petronas, a state-owned petroleum company in Malaysia, bought Star Energy plc, supplier of gas storage equipment, in 2008 so Petronas could store and sell more gas in the EU	Assured supplies in timing and quality; reduced costs of supply	Lack of expertise; over-exposure to end-product in one market	Widening expertise and opportunities for promotion; increased market presence and profitability might increase share price in the long run	Initial costs may damage profitability and therefore share price in the short run
Forward vertical merger	A firm merges with a firm closer to the market or consumers in a production process	Titanic Brewery bought five pubs in Staffordshire, June 2010	Greater access to customers; removal of competing suppliers; better information about the final consumer; prevents the 'hold-up' problem when suppliers refuse to supply in order to achieve their own goals	Lack of expertise; over-exposure to end-product in one market	Widening expertise and opportunities for promotion; increased market presence and profitability might increase share price in the long run	Initial costs may damage profitability and therefore share price in the short run
Vertical demerger	Firms at different stages of the production process are broken up	In July 2015 eBay, an online auction site, demerged PayPal, a payment system, listing its shares separately	Avoids negative attention from competition authorities; decreases; exposure to risk in market as a whole	Cost savings are lost; loss of investment in goodwill, branding and human capital	Narrows expertise and opportunities for promotion	Can focus on core product – scope for specialisation and increased returns to investors
Diversi- fication/ conglo- meration	When firms that are involved in unrelated business areas merge	Microsoft, a software company, merged with Nokia, a mobile phone manufacturer, in April 2014	Spreads the risk; widens brand awareness	Dilution of brand, especially if new lines are failing companies	Increased job security and opportunities to become occupationally mobile	Firm might become unwieldy *too large to function properly*

compete because their average cost will be so much higher at a smaller scale. To be able to compete, the new firm would have to operate on a similar scale to the existing firm, which might result in supply increasing quite significantly and therefore a lowering of price, eroding any potential profits to be made.

Size of the market

If a firm serves a niche market that will not support expansion, there is little scope for growth. For instance, manufacturers of cricket bats or a local grocery store might have expanded as far as their market will allow. In these cases, it may be the case that the firm has a local monopoly and any further expansion will put this at risk. Some small firms may survive on the basis that they are able to provide a personal service that customers prefer and would lose some of their loyal customers if they were to expand.

Lack of resources and access to finance

The owner of the firm may lack the knowledge, expertise or funds needed for expansion. As the firm expands and employs more people, it may encounter a greater level of bureaucracy, such as needing to complete National Insurance returns or having to comply with greater levels of financial regulation, which will either add to its costs or be beyond the managers' level of expertise.

Minimum efficient scale

In some cases a firm might have already exploited **economies of scale** and be operating at the most productively efficient point: that is, the optimum efficiency might have been achieved. Any further increase would result in inefficiencies and in an increase in average cost: in other words, the firm would experience **diseconomies of scale**. Take the case of a family-run restaurant. Any expansion, such as opening another restaurant, may require the hiring of a manager and the training of a chef. The loss of personal managerial control may result in increased costs and eventually losses.

Owner objectives

Expansion may result in increased rewards but perhaps the opportunity cost in terms of lost leisure will be too much for a sole trader and therefore they remain small: in other words, they lack the motivation to expand. This is an example of **satisficing**, where a firm makes just enough profit to stay in business and then allows other motives to take precedence. Some managers may not be willing to undertake the risks that are necessary to expand a business, instead seeking to avoid such expansion. Behavioural economists might try to explain such risk-averse behaviour, but it could come down to something as simple as wishing to avoid taking risks with the family finances, mortgage or savings.

Avoiding attention from potential buyers

The growth of the firm and its increased profits may result in unwanted overtures from larger firms wishing to buy out the sole trader. It is therefore an advantage to remain small and avoid attention.

Knowledge check 5

What is a niche market?

Exam tip

Satisficing behaviour is when a firm aims to make a minimum acceptable level of profit and then pursues other aims.

Tax thresholds and other benefits of remaining small

Small firms are able to access additional training grants and government financial support. For example, firms with profits of less than £10 000 are not liable for corporation tax and firms with turnover of less than £81 000 are not liable for VAT in the UK. Since 2009, the government has supported small firms with a turnover of up to £41 million through the Enterprise Finance Guarantee, which allows smaller firms to access bank loans of between £1000 and £1.2 million, and the government guarantees 75% of the risk of firms being unable to pay back the loan.

Demergers

Reasons for demergers

Some firms may grow too large and experience diseconomies of scale. As a result of the growth of output, the business and managers may lose focus and control over day-to-day management of the firm and therefore long-run average costs may tend to increase. To avoid this, or to reduce the impact of diseconomies of scale, a firm may decide to break up – in other words, to **demerge**. This may then create a number of smaller firms, all able to concentrate on their specialist areas and maximise their own economies of scale and, with that, increase shareholder value and profits. As a result, parts of the business may also be shut, resulting in a loss of jobs.

Impact of demergers on businesses, workers and consumers

Sometimes demergers are required by governments, e.g. on the direction of the Competition and Markets Authority (CMA), because the business is seen to be acting against the public interest. An example in 2014 was when Lloyds TSB was ordered by the European Commission to sell off its TSB part of the business because it was receiving state aid in the wake of its takeover of HBOS in 2009.

The impact on the business is to make it smaller, which might mean it has less control in the market (reduction of market share) and less monopoly power (see pages 33–37). This might make the business less profitable, but it might also make it more profitable if it becomes more efficient (it is likely to sell off its least profitable or its loss-making parts).

Workers are often the main losers when it comes to demergers. Some might be forced to move location: for example, if they are working in the headquarters of a part of a firm that experiences a change in ownership. They might even lose their job if the new owners find they have workers in similar roles already.

Consumers tend to face short-term problems: for example, their bank might change its name and the way it works, or branches might close. But the intended long-term effect, if it has been instigated by the government, is to create more competition in the market and therefore lower prices and more choice for the consumer.

Exam tip

Ensure you know arguments for firms to remain small, which can be used for evaluation when explaining a question about growth of firms.

Knowledge check 6

Is it shareholders or managers who care most about the size of the firm?

Demerger The separation of a larger firm into two or more smaller organisations, often as the un-merging of an earlier merger.

Knowledge check 7

If a firm wants to avoid diseconomies of scale, what should it do? How could this be shown on a cost diagram?

Exam tip

Make sure you know of at least one example of a recent demerger to use as case study material.

Summary

- It is important to know why some firms will grow and to be able to discuss the advantages of growth.
- We have looked at how firms grow, either by joining with another firm in a vertical, horizontal or conglomerate merger, or by internal growth such as through investment in the business itself.
- You must know why some firms remain small – perhaps there are barriers to entry to a variety of industries, a lack of economies of scale, or competitive advantages in staying small (possibly the firm reacts more quickly to change), or they have a better relationship with customers than larger firms do.
- We have also considered why some firms may decide to become smaller through the process of demerger, and some of the issues that arise as a demerger occurs, including the impact on various stakeholders – the advantages of a small but focused firm are set against those of a firm enjoying economies of scale and market power.

▪ Revenues, costs and profits

Revenue

Total revenue

Total revenue (TR), also called turnover or sales revenue, is the amount the firm receives from all its sales over a certain period:

TR = price × quantity

Average revenue

Average revenue (AR), or revenue per unit, is how much people pay per unit (price) and also the demand curve. The formula is:

$$AR = \frac{\text{total revenue}}{\text{quantity}}$$

Marginal revenue

Marginal revenue (MR) is the revenue associated with each additional unit sold, i.e. the change in total revenue from selling one more unit. It is the gradient of the total revenue curve.

Both average revenue and marginal revenue tend to be downward sloping, as in Figure 1 (unless the firm is operating under conditions of perfect competition), and reflect the downward-sloping demand curve and the need for firms to lower prices to increase sales.

Output	Total revenue	Marginal revenue
10	63	–
11	75	12
12	86	11

Knowledge check 8

What is the result of multiplying price and quantity?

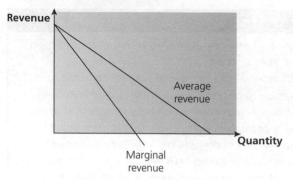

Figure 1 Average and marginal revenue

Therefore, the average revenue curve is also the firm's demand curve. This can be calculated by:

$$\text{Average revenue} = \frac{P \times Q}{Q}$$

Price elasticity of demand and its relationship to revenue concepts

In Theme 1 you will recall coming across the concept of price elasticity of demand (*PED*). There is a relationship between the price elasticity of demand and both the average revenue and marginal revenue curves. If we consider the elasticity of two points on the average revenue curve, we can see that the elasticity changes at different points along the curve.

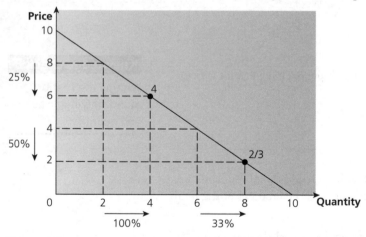

Figure 2 Point price elasticity of demand

In Figure 2 we can see that as the firm lowers prices from £8 to £6 it increases sales from 2 to 4. If we convert these to percentages, we can work out the *PED* for this point.

The fall in price from £8 to £6 is a fall of 25% and the increase in sales from 2 to 4 is a 100% increase in sales. *PED* is: $\dfrac{\text{percentage change in quantity demanded}}{\text{percentage change in price}}$

$$\frac{100\%}{-25\%} = -4$$

Remember that economists ignore the negative sign when calculating the *PED*.

When the price falls further from 4 to 2 there is a 50% fall in price and an increase in sales from 6 to 8, which is an increase of 33%.

$$\frac{33\%}{-50\%} = -2/3$$

From Theme 1 we can recall that an elasticity greater than 1 is said to be relatively price elastic and an elasticity less than 1 is relatively price inelastic. So in this case the top half of the demand curve, where the elasticity is 4, is relatively price elastic and the bottom half of the demand curve, where the elasticity is 2/3, is relatively price inelastic.

We can then apply this information to work out what happens to total revenue when prices are changed on the elastic and inelastic parts of the average revenue curve. In Figure 3 we can see that if prices fall by 10% on the elastic part of the demand curve then sales increase by 20%, which means that the firm is selling proportionately more than the fall in price, so total revenue increases. On the inelastic part of the demand curve, when the firm raises prices by 20% it sees sales fall by only 10% and so although it is selling fewer goods, they are at a proportionately higher price and therefore total revenue increases.

Therefore, in summary we can say that on the elastic part of the demand curve, if the firm lowers prices then total revenue increases and if it raises prices then total revenue falls. If we consider the inelastic part of the demand curve, if the firm lowers prices then it will witness a fall in revenue and if the firm raises prices then it will experience a rise in revenue. This is worth noting when the kinked demand curve is considered on page 33.

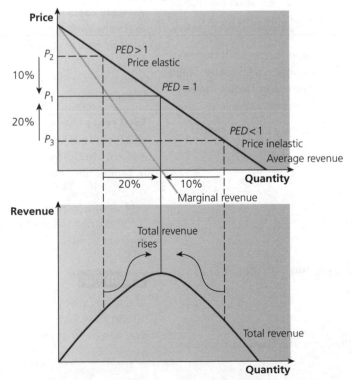

Figure 3 Price elasticity of demand and average, marginal and total revenue

Knowledge check 9

Can you simplify the equation $AR = (P \times Q)/Q$? What does it mean?

Exam tip

If you see a horizontal *AR* and *MR*, the firm is a price taker and operating under conditions of perfect competition. In all other cases, *AR* and *MR* will be downward sloping and *MR* will be twice as steep as *AR*.

Costs

The short and the long run

Before we can draw a cost curve, we must determine which time period we are considering:

- **Short run.** This can be defined as a time period in which at least one factor of production (land, labour, capital or entrepreneurship) is fixed – it cannot be changed even if there is a change in demand. The length of time that this represents will vary for different firms. For example, a pizza delivery firm could probably double in size within a matter of days, but an oil exploration firm might take 20 years because of the geological research and legal costs involved. The explanation of short-run costs is the law of diminishing returns.
- **Long run.** This is defined as a time period in which all the factors of production are variable. The explanation of long-run costs is economies and diseconomies of scale.

Total cost

There are two types of cost:

- **Fixed costs.** These costs do not change with output. Fixed costs can apply only when at least one factor of production (land, labour, capital and entrepreneurship) is fixed. This will be the case in the short run only. For example, an out-of-town supermarket has a fixed supply of available land in the short term. In the future, the supermarket may be able to buy more land adjacent to the site, showing that in the long run, all factors of production are variable. Fixed costs are also known as overheads.
- **Variable costs.** These costs do change with output and can occur in both the short run and the long run. An example might be a firm's raw material costs, which will increase as the firm produces more products. If a car producer makes more cars, it will use more steel.

Taken together, total fixed costs and total variable costs are known as **total costs**.

Average costs

Average fixed cost

Average fixed cost (*AFC*) is calculated as follows:

$$\frac{\text{fixed costs}}{\text{output}}$$

For example, if a firm's fixed costs are £1,000 and output is 100, *AFC* is calculated as follows:

$$AFC = \frac{£1000}{100} = £10 \text{ per unit of output}$$

As output increases, *AFC* will always continue to fall because the fixed cost is being spread across a greater output.

Short-run A time period in which at least one factor of production is fixed.

Long-run A time period when all factors of production are variable.

Fixed costs Costs that do not vary with output – these can occur in the short run only.

Variable costs Costs that vary with output, such as raw material consumption in a manufacturing process.

Total costs These will include all the rewards to the factors of production, i.e. wages (labour), rent (land), interest (capital), normal profit (entrepreneur).

Exam tip

AFC is an 'always falling curve': that is, average fixed costs can never rise.

Average variable cost

Average variable cost (*AVC*) is calculated as follows:

$$\frac{\text{variable costs}}{\text{output}}$$

For example, if a firm's total variable cost is £5000 and it produces 100 units, *AVC* is calculated as follows:

$$AVC = \frac{£5,000}{100} = £50 \text{ per unit of output}$$

The average total cost (usually abbreviated to *AC*) is equal to *AFC* + *AVC*, which in this case is £10 + £50 = £60 at an output of 100.

Average cost (*AC*) or average total cost (*ATC*) is found by adding *AFC* and *AVC*, or by dividing total cost by the quantity produced.

Marginal cost

Marginal cost (*MC*) is the change in total cost when one additional unit of output is produced. It is the gradient of the total cost curve, $\Delta TC/\Delta Q$ – the change in total cost divided by a one-unit change in output.

Output	Total cost	Marginal cost
0	£100	–
1	£119	£19
2	£135	£16

As output increases from 0 to 1, the total cost rises by £19. This is the marginal cost.

Marginal cost always goes through the minimum point of the average variable cost and average total cost curves (as in Figure 4). This can be explained using some marginal analysis. If we can imagine that the average height of a group of people is 6 feet and we add some people who are 5 feet tall, then the average height will fall. This is because the marginal height of the class, in other words the height of the next person added, is 5 feet, which is less than the average height. Therefore if the marginal unit is below the average unit, the average will fall. If the marginal height of the next person added was more than 6 feet, the average height would increase. The same applies to the cost of production. If the marginal cost is greater than the average cost, the average must be rising. The only time that the average is not falling or rising is when the marginal cost is equal to the average cost and the average has stopped falling and has yet to start rising.

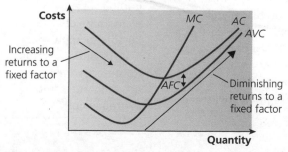

Figure 4 Short-run average costs

Average cost Average cost per unit of output.

Marginal cost Change in total costs when one more unit of output is produced.

Exam tip

You can abbreviate marginal cost as $\Delta TC/\Delta Q$, but never forget the ΔQ part. Many miss out the 'change in' sign in the denominator.

Knowledge check 10

Why does *MC* cross *AC* at its lowest point?

Exam tip

The gap between the average total cost and the average variable cost gets smaller as output rises. *AC* = *AFC* + *AVC*. So as output rises, *AC* is nearer in value to *AVC* because average fixed cost is always falling as output rises and *AVC* starts to rise because of the law of diminishing returns.

Deriving the short-run average cost curve

The average total cost and average variable cost curves slope downwards because of increasing returns to a fixed factor. In other words, as greater inputs are added to a fixed factor such as a shop or factory floor, the firm will increase output at a faster rate and therefore average costs will fall. However, beyond the lowest point of the *AC* and *AVC*, the firm begins to experience diminishing returns to a fixed factor and therefore, as more factors of production are added to a fixed factor, they start to add less than the last to total output and the *AC* and *AVC* start to increase.

Economies and diseconomies of scale

In the long run, all costs are variable and average costs are explained by economies and diseconomies of scale (see Figure 5).

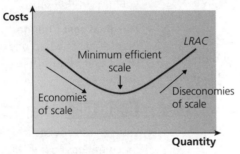

Figure 5 Economies and diseconomies of scale

Economies of scale

Internal economies of scale

Internal **economies of scale** are falling long-run average costs associated with an increase in output for an individual firm.

Types of economies of scale include:

- **Financial economies.** As a firm grows, it is better able to access loans at low cost. Banks will be more willing to lend as there is less risk associated with the transaction.
- **Risk-bearing economies.** As the firm expands, it is better able to develop a range of products and a wider customer base to spread risk and minimise the impact of any downturn.
- **Marketing economies.** As a firm expands its product range, it is able to use any central brand marketing to advertise the range at little extra cost and therefore spread this across a wider range of goods and decrease long-run average cost. For example, if Mars advertises its chocolate bars, it is also indirectly advertising its ice cream with no additional cost by developing brand awareness.
- **Managerial economies.** As a firm expands, it is in a position to employ specialist managers in finance, sales or operations and therefore increase productivity and decrease long-run average costs.

Economies of scale
A fall in long-run average costs as output increases.

Exam tip

You must know a number of types of economies of scale and be able to apply these in different scenarios. Remember they are long-run falling average costs.

■ **Increased dimensions.** A haulage company, for example, is able to expand the quantities it carries by doubling the dimensions and therefore the costs, but in consequence it increases the volume eight-fold (see Figure 6). This is a factor contributing to increased globalisation as firms are better able to transport goods around the world at low cost (see Theme 4).

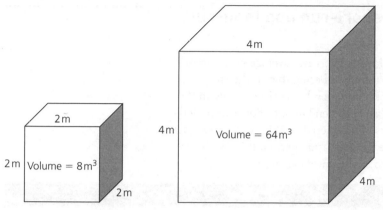

Figure 6 Increased dimensions

External economies of scale

Internal economies of scale occur when an individual firm expands, whereas external economies of scale have an impact on the entire industry and therefore lower the long-run average cost curve, as illustrated in Figure 7.

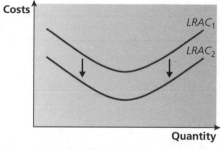

Figure 7 External economies of scale

An industry may benefit as a result of innovations produced by other firms and therefore all firms will see their average cost of production fall.

Retailers located close to each other are able to benefit from the development of new roads and transport links, which lower the long-run average costs of all the firms.

A group of small businesses is able to share administrative and secretarial facilities and therefore enjoy lower long-run costs per unit.

Diseconomies of scale

A firm may experience **diseconomies of scale** if it grows too large and moves beyond its minimum efficient scale. Diseconomies of scale may result from a breakdown in communication or other managerial difficulties and will lead to long-run average costs

Diseconomies of scale
An increase in long-run average costs as output increases. This is often associated with managerial difficulties.

increasing as output increases. This may occur when a firm merges with another or when a firm grows internally and management lacks the experience necessary to maintain managerial focus and control. Such expansion may also result in a lack of co-ordination between departments within the firm, leading to greater levels of productive inefficiency, waste and an increase in long-run average costs.

Knowledge check 11

If a firm is experiencing falling diseconomies of scale, are costs per unit rising or falling?

The relationship between the short-run and long-run average cost curves

The long-run average cost curve is made up of many short-run average cost curves joined together at their lowest points. It is worth remembering that in the short run the firm is constrained by at least one factor of production being fixed, while in the long run all factors of production are variable, so at the end of one short-run period the firm will be able to change all of its factors of production and in turn enter a new short run. All of these short runs make up the long-run time period. It is for this reason that the $LRAC$ is sometimes referred to as the envelope curve.

Summary

- In the short run at least one factor is fixed, but in the long run all factors are variable.
- Fixed costs do not change with output and therefore exist only in the short run, along with any variable cost. If fixed costs increase, there is no change in marginal cost because fixed costs do not change with output and marginal cost is the increase in costs when output changes. In the long run, all costs are variable.
- $TC = TFC + TVC$ and $AC = TC/Q$ are crucial cost equations and you must understand how MC relates to these. $TR = P \times Q$, and $AR = PQ/Q$ or just P or the demand curve. You must understand how MR relates to these.

■ Business objectives

The main business objectives

Firms are assumed to be profit maximisers, but sometimes they may opt to satisfy different objectives such as revenue maximisation or sales maximisation.

Profit maximisation

Profit maximisation occurs at the output level where supernormal profits are at their greatest (or losses are at their lowest). This occurs where marginal cost is equal to marginal revenue ($MC = MR$), but while this is a necessary condition, it is not sufficient. Marginal cost must also be rising.

Profit maximisation
Occurs where $MC = MR$. It is where the firm maximises profits or minimises losses.

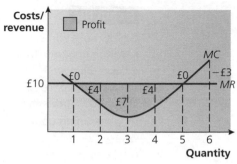

Figure 8 Profit maximisation

In Figure 8, at an output of 1, marginal profit is zero: in other words, there is no profit from the last unit sold. The difference between this output and the next time we have a marginal profit of zero (5 units sold) is that at an output of 5 the firm is maximising its profits. This is because we can see each unit sold between 1 and 5 is adding to total profit. The data from Figure 8 are converted into a table below.

When the fifth unit is sold, marginal cost equals marginal revenue, and as we know that marginal cost is rising, then the next unit sold (the sixth) will cause marginal cost to rise above marginal revenue. The sixth unit sold results in a marginal loss of £3 and therefore a fall in total profit from the peak of £15 to £12.

Therefore, firms will seek to equate marginal cost with marginal revenue to maximise profits.

Output	Marginal revenue	Marginal cost	Marginal profit	Total profit
1	£10	£10	£0	£0
2	£10	£6	£4	£4
3	£10	£3	£7	£11
4	£10	£6	£4	£15
5	£10	£10	£0	£15
6	£10	£13	−£3	£12

When evaluating profit maximisation, consider whether the local coffee shop knows the marginal cost of a cup of coffee. Furthermore, what would it do if it knew that level of output? Would it stop selling because the next item would result in a fall in total profit? Some firms, then, look to other objectives.

Revenue maximisation

Revenue maximisation occurs when a firm seeks to make as much revenue as possible. Firms are willing to sell products until the last unit sold adds nothing to total revenue, knowing that the next unit sold will reduce revenue: that is, they sell until the marginal revenue is zero. This can be illustrated by the diagram in Figure 9.

Exam tip

When $MC = MR$, no more profit can be made, either by increasing or by decreasing output. The marginal profit is zero.

Knowledge check 12

The formula for profit maximisation is $MC = MR$. Why does the firm stop producing any more here?

Revenue maximisation
When a firm maximises total revenue. This occurs where marginal revenue = 0.

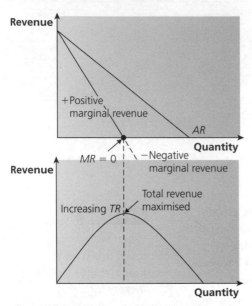

Figure 9 Revenue maximisation where $MR = 0$

Exam tip

On any question on revenue maximisation, draw a diagram showing the parabola-shaped TR curve with its peak lining up with where the MR crosses the horizontal axis. Mark on $MR = 0$.

Figure 9 shows that, as the firm expands output, the marginal revenue declines. While marginal revenue is positive, it continues to add to total revenue; it is only when it passes zero and becomes negative that total revenue starts to decline.

Sales maximisation

Sales maximisation occurs when a firm attempts to sell as much as it can without making a loss. That is, it sells as much as it can subject to the constraint of making normal profits. This occurs where average cost equals average revenue (see Figure 10).

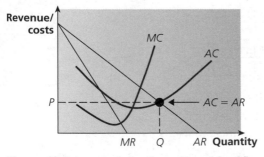

Figure 10 Sales maximisation where $AC = AR$

Firms may embark on revenue or sales maximisation in an effort to gain market share or drive a rival out of the industry. Prices are lower than under perfect competition and output is higher.

Other motives for firms

Governments may seek to ensure that firms operate at the **allocatively efficient** point (see Figure 11). This is where price equals marginal cost. In other words, the price paid for a good is equal to the cost of the factors of production used to manufacture the last unit.

Knowledge check 13

Why might a firm choose to operate at its revenue maximisation point?

Sales maximisation
When a firm maximises sales of its output while achieving normal profit.

Exam tip

Do not confuse sales maximisation, $AR = AC$, with sales *revenue* maximisation, $MR = 0$ (which is what is referred to in this guide as 'revenue maximisation' – see page 21). Remember that sales maximisation is the highest level of sales given that the firm must make normal profit. It is also called output maximisation.

Allocative efficiency
Producing at a point where the price of a good is equal to the marginal cost of production.

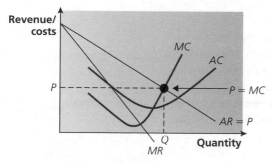

Figure 11 Allocative efficiency where $P = MC$

Other motives include **satisficing**. This is an important behavioural theory that you need to know for this theme. It means making just enough profit to keep stakeholders happy, allowing for other motives then to be pursued. Stakeholders are people who have a vested interest in the firm. They include shareholders, employees, managers, customers, suppliers, government and the trade unions.

Another motive is long-run profit maximisation with short-term increased market dominance as a primary motive, which may lead to higher profits over time.

Strategies to gain market share or increase profitability

Pricing strategies

Firms can decide to adopt a number of strategies designed to gain market share or increase profitability in the long run while sacrificing short-run profits. In the exam you are likely to be asked to write a short essay on what a firm, discussed in the data, could do to improve sales, market share or profits, and this is a good place to start your answer.

- **Predatory pricing:** pricing below costs to drive out other firms. In the short run the firm makes a loss, but as the other firms leave, the prices are raised to higher levels than would have been possible with competition. This is an anti-competitive practice and can lead to fines being imposed by the competition authorities.

- **Limit pricing:** pricing at a level low enough to discourage entry of new firms: that is, ensuring that the price of the good is below that which a new firm entering the industry would be able to sustain. This exploits the economies of scale that an incumbent firm has and is not necessarily illegal in the UK.

In the short run, both limit and predatory pricing will seem to benefit the consumer by giving them low prices. However, when the firm has managed to drive rival firms out of the industry and gained monopoly power, it will be able to raise prices, reducing the consumer surplus and reducing consumer choice.

Other pricing strategies firms might use, apart from profit maximising, are cost-plus pricing (making a fixed percentage mark-up on average costs), price discrimination (discussed on pages 35–36) and discount pricing such as 'buy one get one free'. These often have a good practical rationale and can lead to greater consumer loyalty, thereby increasing long-run profits.

Satisficing A combination of two words: 'satisfying' (keeping people happy) and 'sufficing' (just enough). So it means 'doing just enough to make certain stakeholders are happy'.

Non-price competition

As an alternative to limit pricing and predatory pricing, firms may embark on non-price competition in order to increase sales or profit. This is particularly evident where price competition might lead to price wars. Any action by a firm that does not involve changing price comes under this category, including marketing strategies such as advertising (also including placing the product in the hands of celebrities), increased investment in branding (including measures to increase brand loyalty, such as loyalty cards), packaging (for instance, including free gifts or prizes), after-care/customer service/warranties, product development, quality and innovation, and mergers/acquisitions to remove competition. Here you can also include 'buy one get one free' as it is a commonly used marketing technique to attempt to increase consumer loyalty.

The aim of non-pricing strategies is to shift the average revenue (demand) curve to the right (as shown in Figure 12) or to prevent it from falling as other firms try to increase their market share. The cost of the advertising must be below the increase in supernormal profit if it is to be of any benefit.

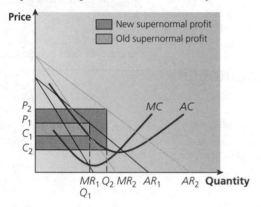

Figure 12 Shift in average and marginal revenue and impact on profits

Do non-pricing strategies work? It may be the case that other firms will also increase their advertising or copy the innovations being introduced, and spending large sums of money on an advertising campaign is no guarantee of success. When evaluating, it is always worth asking whether the firm has enough money to back up any planned non-price competition strategy, how long it will take to work, and indeed whether or not it will work at all, especially in the face of the actions of rival firms.

> **Exam tip**
>
> The aim of non-pricing strategies is to increase demand for the good being sold and to reduce the price elasticity of demand by reducing the availability of substitutes, without changing price.

> **Exam tip**
>
> You must be very careful to explain the long run when analysing pricing and non-pricing strategies as 'ways to increase profits' because in the short run there might be a decrease in profits.

Summary

- Firms are assumed to be profit maximisers.
- Profit maximisation occurs where $MC = MR$ and marginal cost is rising.
- Firms will pursue other objectives such as revenue or sales maximisation.
- Revenue maximisation occurs where $MR = 0$.
- Sales maximisation occurs where a firm can sell as much as it can without making a loss – this is where $AC = AR$.
- Managers may seek to satisfice rather than profit maximise.
- Some firms will pursue other pricing or non-pricing strategies.

Market structures

The characteristics of four models of market sellers are required for Theme 3, as well as one model of market buyers (monopsony). The spectrum of the selling models is shown in Figure 13, ranging according to the number of sellers in the market.

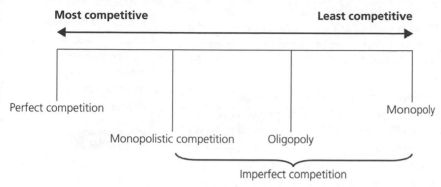

Figure 13 Competition spectrum

Firms operate in a market structure and the prices and output they set are determined largely by the nature of competition in the market.

Calculation of *n*-firm concentration ratios and their significance

When considering market structure, it is always useful to consider how many firms dominate the market. In highly concentrated markets few firms dominate – for example, the mobile phone industry or the UK banking sector. The **concentration ratio** can be defined as the market share controlled by the *n* largest firms. For example, the four-firm concentration ratio is the market share controlled by the four largest firms in an industry. An oligopoly would be highly concentrated and a monopolistically competitive market would have a low concentration ratio.

Knowledge check 14

What does highly concentrated mean in the context of a market structure?

Exam tip

A useful rule to decide whether a market is an oligopoly is a handy **f**-rule: if **f**ive or **f**ewer firms have **50**% market share, the market is highly concentrated and likely to have the characteristics of an oligopoly.

Characteristics \ Market model	Perfect competition	Monopolistic competition	Oligopoly	Monopoly
Number of firms/market concentration	Many small firms/low concentration	Many small firms/low concentration	A few large firms dominate/high concentration	One firm has 100% concentration ratio
Type of product	Homogeneous	Similar	Some distinct characteristics, such as PC and Mac	Unique
Knowledge	Perfect	Imperfect	Imperfect	Imperfect
Barriers to entry/exit	None	Low	High	High
Price-setting powers	Price taker	Some degree of price-setting power in local market	Significant price-setting powers, but interdependent	Price maker

Summary of the key characteristics of market structures

Efficiency

- **Productive efficiency** occurs at the lowest cost per unit of output, or the lowest point of the average cost curve. The firm is producing as much as possible relative to inputs. It is where the marginal cost intersects the average cost.
- **Allocative efficiency** occurs when the cost of production and the demands of consumers are taken into account to maximise welfare. Firms will charge a price equal to the marginal cost ($P = MC$) of manufacturing the good. It is where the price charged for the last unit (the amount people are prepared to pay) is equal to the cost of making the last unit, so net welfare falls if any more units are produced. It is also called **welfare maximisation**.
- **Dynamic efficiency** looks at how changes in technology and productive techniques over time will increase the productive potential of a firm. This is very distinct from productive and allocative efficiencies which are assumed to be static.
- **X-inefficiency** occurs when the average cost is higher than the lowest possible average cost: in other words, the firm operates above its AC curve. This can happen in highly concentrated markets, such as monopoly (pages 33–37) and oligopoly (pages 30–33), where firms are able to make supernormal profits and have an AR that is greater than their AC, thus reducing the need or desire to lower AC and decrease x-inefficiency.

Perfect competition

Characteristics of perfect competition

Number of firms	Many small firms
Type of product	Homogeneous (exactly the same)
Knowledge	Perfect knowledge – this doesn't mean the firm knows everything about rival firms' price and output decisions. Rather, it means the firm has access to this information, including the latest technology and techniques and information on who makes supernormal profits
Barriers to entry/exit	None
Price-setting powers	None – perfectly competitive firms take the price set by the market. They are known as price takers (see Figure 14)

Characteristics of perfect competition

The characteristics required for **perfect competition** suggest that there are few industries that approximate to the model of perfect competition. These include the market for foreign currency, where there are low barriers to entry, price takers (the price of currency sold is determined by the market), many small firms and homogeneous goods (currencies are the same whoever sells them), and the market for agricultural goods such as carrots.

Productive efficiency
Occurs at the lowest point on the average cost curve. This is where average cost is at its lowest.

Allocative efficiency
Producing at a point where the price of a good is equal to the marginal cost of production.

Exam tip

Many types of examination question can be asked on efficiency – it may be discussed in the context of the theory of the firm or government intervention. Make sure you apply efficiency to the context and use diagrams to explain where you can.

Perfect competition
A market where a large number of small firms co-exist, selling homogeneous products. Normal profits are achieved in the long run because there are no barriers to entry to protect the market share of those firms that make supernormal profits in the short run.

Profit-maximising equilibrium in the short run and the long run

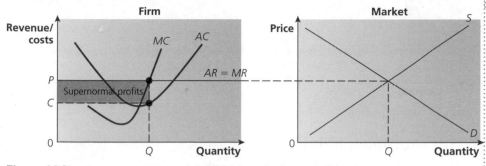

Figure 14 Short-run supernormal profits in perfect competition

In the diagram shown in Figure 14, the firm is taking the industry- or market-determined price (P). This is above the firm's average cost at the profit-maximising output of $MC = MR$. Therefore, the firm is making supernormal profits, as indicated on the diagram.

From the diagram we can see that the firm is operating in the short run. Perfectly competitive firms cannot maintain supernormal profits in the long run, because rival firms will see that these supernormal profits are being made (because of perfect knowledge) and enter the industry (no barriers to entry). The market-supply curve will shift to the right and the price will fall (see Figure 15), until all the supernormal profits are competed away and the firms make normal profits in the long run.

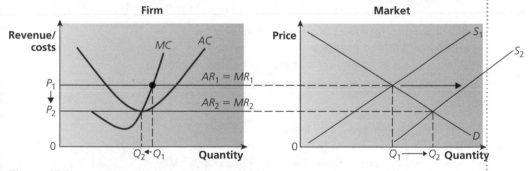

Figure 15 Competition causing prices to fall in long-run perfect competition

Figure 15 shows the market output increase from Q_1 to Q_2 and the firm reacts to the resulting drop in price from P_1 to P_2 by reducing output to Q_2.

In the long run, a perfectly competitive firm will always make normal profits only, any supernormal profits having been competed away and the losses removed by firms leaving the industry. This is known as the **long-run equilibrium** (Figure 16).

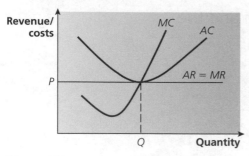

Figure 16 Long-run equilibrium in perfect competition

Short-run and long-run shutdown points

The shutdown point for a perfectly competitive firm (and all firms for that matter) occurs when the firm is not covering average variable costs. It may be feasible for a firm to make a loss in the short run, as long as it covers the variable cost of making the good and therefore makes a contribution to the fixed costs. This is illustrated in the table below by comparing the example of a firm that shuts down and has to pay its fixed costs with a firm that stays open and therefore makes a contribution to fixed costs.

If the firm were to close and produce nothing:	If the firm were to remain open and produce 10 000 units.
Quantity produced = 0 Fixed costs = £100 000 **Loss = £100 000**	Quantity produced = 10 000 Fixed costs = £100 000 Price per unit (average revenue) = £10 ∴ **Total revenue** ($P \times Q$) = £10 × 10 000 = **£100 000** Variable cost per unit (AVC) = £7 Total variable costs ($AVC \times Q$) = £7 × 10 000 = £70 000 **Total cost** is made up of fixed costs and variable costs: i.e. £100 000 + £70 000 = **£170 000** **Loss** = total revenue − total cost = £100 000 − £170 000 = **£70 000**
Thus the loss by staying open is £70 000, which is less than if the firm had closed and incurred the £100 000 fixed cost.	

Therefore, by remaining open, the firm is able to reduce its loss to £70,000 and it makes a contribution of £30,000 towards fixed costs. At this level of output, where the marginal revenue crosses the marginal cost, the firm will remain open, as it is making a contribution towards fixed costs. In Figure 17 the firm will continue to operate where marginal cost is above average variable cost (e.g. at Q_1, Q_2 or Q_3) but will shut down if it cannot cover average variable cost.

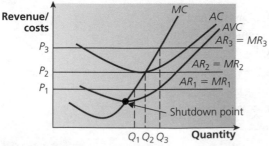

Figure 17 Supply curve for a perfectly competitive firm

Monopolistic competition

Characteristics of monopolistic competition

Monopolistically competitive firms have many of the characteristics of firms operating under conditions of perfect competition *except* they are able to set price to a limited extent because the products they produce are not exactly the same, customers have some loyalty in a market, and the demand curve is not perfectly price elastic. Examples include restaurants, hairdressers and nail bars. The firms are easy to set up, have some local loyalty from returning customers, but do not enjoy supernormal profits in the long run. They are closed down quickly if demand falls.

Number of firms	Many small firms
Type of product	Similar goods, slightly differentiated possibly through, among other things, quality, branding or advertising
Knowledge	Imperfect knowledge about rival firms' price and output decisions but firms will be able to identify when supernormal profits are being made
Barriers to entry/exit	Low
Price-setting powers	Firms can set price to an extent because they are producing goods that are slightly different from those of rival firms

Characteristics of monopolistic competition

Profit-maximising equilibrium in the short run and the long run

In the short run, a monopolistically competitive firm can make supernormal profits, as illustrated in Figure 18. As with all market structures apart from perfect competition, a monopolistically competitive firm need not operate at the productively efficient (i.e. lowest point on the average cost curve) or allocatively efficient (i.e. where price = marginal cost) levels of output.

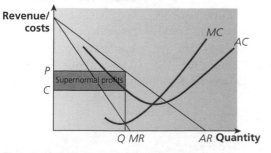

Figure 18 Supernormal profits in short-run monopolistic competition

However, as with perfect competition, a monopolistically competitive firm cannot maintain supernormal profits in the long run due to the near perfect knowledge that allows firms to identify the profits to be made, and the low barriers to entry that allow firms to enter the market and compete profits away. It is for these reasons that the long-run position for a monopolistically competitive firm is in the equilibrium depicted in Figure 19.

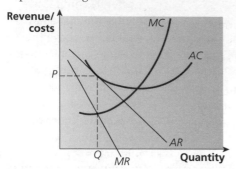

Figure 19 Long-run equilibrium in monopolistic competition

It is also true that monopolistically competitive firms do not make losses in the long run because, as in perfect competition, there are very low barriers to exit, which means that should firms be making losses they will leave the industry rather than try to persevere in the long run. They are unlikely to have sufficient cash reserves to be able to justify the pursuit of long-run profits as a motive.

> **Exam tip**
>
> The diagram for monopolistic competition in the long run is difficult to draw because the *AR* and *AC* are at a tangent at the same output as *MC* = *MR*. It is worthwhile adding the *AC* curve last when you draw the diagram, making sure that you line up the points, as the examiner will check carefully for this.

Oligopoly

Characteristics of oligopoly

Oligopoly exists where a few, interdependent firms dominate the market. Interdependence means that the actions of one firm in the industry will impact on the other firms in the industry: for example, if one firm were to lower its prices, this could force other firms to react in the same way, otherwise they would lose market share. This sort of market structure typically plays host to collusive behaviour among the main firms. Examples of oligopolies include the brewing industry, pharmaceuticals, food and confectionery manufacturers and petrol retailers.

Number of firms	A few large firms dominate
Type of product	Goods with some similar characteristics but brand loyalty tends to be strong
Knowledge	Imperfect knowledge about rival firms' price and output decisions
Barriers to entry/exit	High
Price-setting powers	Oligopolies can set price but may decide to agree price-fixing deals with rivals to avoid price competition

Characteristics of oligopoly

> **Knowledge check 16**
>
> Why do firms under monopolistic competition stay in business in the long run, given that they cannot make supernormal profits?

> **Exam tip**
>
> The most common mistake in Theme 3 is to think monopolistic competition is similar to monopoly. In fact its characteristics are so similar to perfect competition that it is often referred to as 'imperfect competition', in the sense that it's not quite perfect, just as you might buy imperfect clothes – you expect them to be very similar to the standard ones, with just a small defect.

> **Oligopoly** A market dominated by a few large firms – often associated with interdependence and collusion.

Competition in oligopolies

With only a few firms dominating an industry (i.e. a high concentration ratio), firms will tend to avoid price competition. This happens because if one firm were to lower prices, others would follow, and although they might gain some additional sales, this would be at the cost of lost revenue from the **price war** that would ensue. Therefore an oligopoly is also characterised by non-price competition (see page 24).

Reasons for collusive and non-collusive behaviour

Collusion can be defined as an agreement between two or more firms to limit competition and therefore divide the market, set prices or output, and increase the welfare gains of the firms concerned to the detriment of other firms and consumers. Most collusion is illegal due to its restrictive nature and its impact on firms and consumers.

Overt and tacit collusion

There are two types of collusion that take place. The first is **overt collusion**, where firms openly fix prices, output, marketing or the sharing out of customers. An extreme form of overt collusion is forming a cartel, which is a formal agreement between firms to act together, as in the case of the sugar cartel that operated in the USA between 1934 and 1974, but cartels are illegal in the EU and many other countries.

The other type of collusion is **tacit collusion**, which is quiet or 'behind the scenes'. This may be implicit co-operation and involve no spoken agreement. The result of tacit collusion is the same as with overt collusion – the firms do not compete with each other or prices are higher than they would otherwise be: that is, there is **price fixing**. Tacit collusion may take the form of a collection of firms avoiding competition and following the actions of a market leader, known as a price leader. This type of collusion is also illegal in most countries and can result in firms being fined or executives being jailed for their actions.

> **Exam tip**
>
> Overt collusion is **open** – it is an agreement between firms to collaborate in some way to restrict competition. Tacit collusion is quiet, unspoken or unwritten. It may be **implied**, or involve firms operating according to some pattern that has never been agreed but has come into effect.

There is always a temptation to break an agreement either to maximise a firm's sales by lowering prices and catching a rival unaware or to gain immunity from prosecution by acting as a whistle-blower and informing the competition authorities about any collusion agreement.

Game theory

This can be illustrated in a simple game theory 2 × 2 matrix, illustrated in Figure 20.

Let us assume that there are two firms, called Adrian and Juju, in an industry. It is clear that if Adrian and Juju collude, they will be able to make profits of £100 million each by setting prices at a high level (Box A). This collusion will result in the two firms collaborating to maximise their combined profits. However, they each know that they can increase their individual profits by lowering prices and breaking any collusive agreement, so obtaining £120 million while the other firm keeps higher prices as agreed and ends up with profits of only £50 million (Boxes B and C). This is known as the **maximax strategy** because it seeks to maximise the firm's maximum payoff.

As a result of neither firm trusting the other, they will therefore both adopt the low-price strategy, trying to do so before the other does, and they will end up with £80 million (Box D), which is a worse outcome than if they had colluded and set a high price, but better than if they had continued to pursue a high price strategy while the other firm lowered its prices. This suggests that due to a lack of trust between firms, any collusive agreement is likely to be broken. This is referred to as the **maximin strategy** because it maximises the firm's minimum payoff.

Examples of game theory include the prisoner's dilemma, which can be used to explain the reaction of two prisoners lacking trust and pursuing their own self-interest in the same way as we have considered the reaction of two firms.

		Adrian	
		High price	**Low price**
Juju	**High price**	**A** Each gets £100m	**B** Juju gets £50m; Adrian gets £120m
	Low price	**C** Juju gets £120m; Adrian gets £50m	**D** Each gets £80m

Figure 20 Game theory 2 × 2 matrix

Another way to illustrate behaviour of oligopolies is to use the kinked demand curve (Figure 21). It shows the price rigidity that exists in many markets and the asymmetric reaction by other firms when one firm raises or lowers its price. It also suggests that firms will not break any collusive agreement as they can see that the outcome will be a price war that is of no benefit to either party.

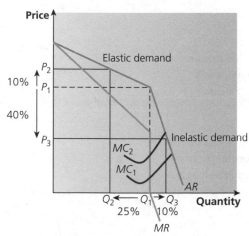

Figure 21 The kinked demand curve

The kinked demand curve illustrates why firms will tend to fix prices at a certain level. If a firm decides to raise prices above P_1 to P_2, it will **be operating** on the **price elastic** part of its kinked demand curve. This is because other firms will not respond and consumers will switch away from the firm raising its price. In Figure 21, a rise in price of the good of 10% will result in a fall in demand of 25%. This means that the firm will experience a decrease in total revenue (price × quantity) after raising its prices.

However, if the firm decided to lower the price to P_3, other firms in the market would follow suit and a price war would ensue, meaning that none of the firms would gain a significant increase in their market share. Therefore the demand for the good is relatively **price inelastic** in relation to a price fall. As the price of the good falls by 40%, the quantity demanded rises by only 10%, which means that the firm will be faced with a decrease in total revenue after lowering its prices.

This suggests that the firm is best keeping its prices at P_1 because either raising or lowering price leads to a fall in revenue. This can be used to explain **sticky prices** – the observation that many shops charge the same amount for some things as their competitors and the prices do not change much over time. It might look like collusion, but here is a reason to argue that it is not.

Monopoly

Characteristics of monopoly

A **monopoly** is the sole supplier of a good or service. The firm is able to set prices and output and to maximise profits. It is known as a price maker.

Number of firms	One
Type of product	Unique
Knowledge	Imperfect knowledge. Potential rival firms will not know the incumbent firm's pricing and output strategy
Barriers to entry/exit	High
Price-setting powers	Price maker

Characteristics of monopoly

Profit-maximising equilibrium

As a result of high barriers to entry, monopolists can set high prices to maximise profits without fear that another firm could enter the industry. It is for this reason that many governments will intervene to prevent the development of monopolies and ensure that competition is maintained in some form. Monopolies are also often accused of being **x-inefficient**. This refers to their tendency to allow costs to rise when there is no threat of a more efficient firm undercutting prices, and their being less inclined to innovate and develop new products because they have no need to maintain an edge over competitors. They may make supernormal profits (see Figure 22) at the expense of consumer surplus and are neither productively nor allocatively efficient (see page 26).

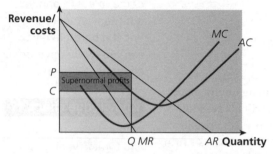

Figure 22 Supernormal profits in a monopoly market structure

Comparing monopoly with perfect competition

	Monopoly	Perfect competition
Profit maximisers	Yes	Yes
Allocatively efficient	No	Yes
Productively efficient	No	Yes
Price	Prices are higher under monopoly compared with perfect competition	Prices are lower under perfect competition compared with monopoly
Quantity	Quantity is lower under monopoly compared with perfect competition	Quantity is higher under perfect competition compared with monopoly

Costs and benefits of monopoly to firms, consumers, employees and suppliers

Disadvantages of monopoly power	Advantages of monopoly power
Supernormal profit means: ■ less incentive to be efficient and to develop new products ■ the existence of resources to protect market dominance by raising barriers to entry and preventing new competition – this will allow the monopolist to exploit its position by allowing it to exert pressure on any suppliers that might rely on it.	Supernormal profit means: ■ finance for investment to maintain competitive edge ■ firms can create reserves to overcome short-term difficulties, giving stability to employment ■ funds for research and development.

Disadvantages of monopoly power	Advantages of monopoly power
Monopoly power means: ■ higher prices and lower output for domestic consumers.	Monopoly power means: ■ firms will have the financial power to match large overseas competitors.
Monopolies may waste resources by undertaking cross-subsidisation, using profits from one sector to finance losses in another sector and employing more labour.	Cross-subsidisation may lead to an increased range of goods or services available to the consumer: for example, the provision of services that are loss-making but provide an external benefit, e.g. rural bus services.
Monopolists may undertake price discrimination to raise producer surplus and reduce consumer surplus.	Price discrimination may raise the firm's total revenue to a point that allows the survival of a product or service.
Monopolists do not produce at the most productively efficient point of output (i.e. at the lowest point of the average cost curve).	Monopolists may be able to take advantage of economies of scale, which means that average costs may be lower than those of a competitive firm at its most efficient position. This is especially the case when there is a natural monopoly (see pages 36–37).
Monopolists can be complacent and develop inefficiencies.	There are few permanent monopolies and the supernormal profit opportunities act as an incentive for rival firms to break down the monopoly through a process of creative destruction, i.e. breaking the monopoly by product development and innovation and therefore bypassing any barriers to entry.
Monopolies may lead to a misallocation of resources by setting prices above marginal cost, so that price is above the opportunity cost of providing the good, i.e. price ≠ marginal cost.	Monopolists can avoid undesirable duplication of services.

Price discrimination

Price discrimination occurs when a firm sells the same product in different markets with differing elasticities at different prices. This is used by a firm with monopoly power to increase profits and to reduce consumer surplus and is possible because of high barriers to entry and exit.

Price discrimination will be successful under three conditions:
■ There are high barriers to entry and a degree of monopoly power.
■ There are at least two separate markets with differing price elasticities of demand.
■ The markets can be kept separate at a cost that is lower than the gain in profits. This is to prevent resale (arbitrage) between the markets.

In practice you are unlikely to see perfect price discrimination and the model you will be required to use is third-degree price discrimination. Here firms can use different prices based on regional, consumer-age or time-of-use differences. Examples of this type of price discrimination include the sale of child and adult railway tickets and the sale of peak and off-peak telephone, electricity and gas services. Lunchtime menus, airline tickets and retail outlets often demonstrate this. The diagram to use is Figure 23. The firm splits the market into relatively elastic and relatively inelastic demand, selling the output at different prices to the two markets and keeping these separate. In this example we assume that the firm faces constant average and marginal costs and has managed to identify two separate markets with differing elasticities. When the firm maximises profit in each market, it is able to make more supernormal profits than if the markets remained as one.

Price discrimination
The sale of the same good to two different markets at different prices. To do this a firm must be a monopolist able to identify two different groups and keep them separate.

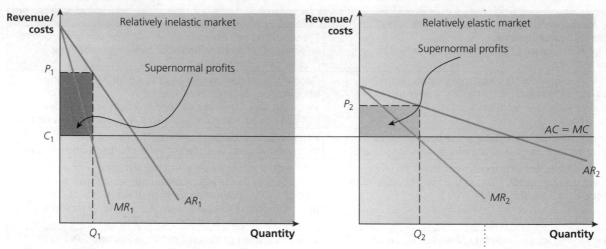

Figure 23 Third-degree price discrimination

Natural monopoly

A natural monopoly exists when an industry can support only one firm. This is typical of an industry that has high **sunk costs** and requires large levels of output to exploit economies of scale.

The introduction of competition, perhaps by some government agency, will not be possible in the long run, as neither of the competing firms would be able to obtain sufficient market share to ensure that it was best able to exploit economies of scale. Any new firm would experience both significant start-up costs, establishing the necessary infrastructure, and long-run losses as it tried to compete with the existing suppliers.

Natural monopolies exist in the supply of water, gas, the rail industry and electricity, where there are high start-up and infrastructure costs. The costs of establishing a competing firm will outweigh any economic or social benefit that might materialise. This is illustrated in Figure 24, where it is clear that the firm operates at the profit-maximising point when it reaches an output of 1 million. Should the market be opened to competition and both firms take an equal share of the market, i.e. 500,000, they will each make a loss. If one of the firms gained a greater market share then it might be able to survive, but this would be at the expense of the other firm, which would eventually fail, returning the industry to a monopoly situation.

Sunk costs Costs that a firm cannot recover on exit, such as advertising.

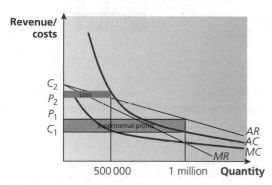

Figure 24 Natural monopoly

The term 'natural monopoly' is new to this exam. Monopoly features as a very important model in microeconomics. This form of monopoly can be used to evaluate whether monopolies are in fact unavoidable and whether they are best left as monopolies and regulated rather than being forced to compete.

Monopsony

Monopsony power exists when sellers face powerful buyers. For example, if an individual wishes to work in emergency healthcare in the UK, then the sole buyer of such employees is the National Health Service. A number of firms could act together (collude) to increase buying power. In the supermarket industry, for example, the major retailers may join together to exploit their suppliers and ensure that the supermarkets are able to get the best possible price for their goods. A farmer faced with the choice of selling everything produced to the supermarket, or selling goods in the open market, usually opts to sell to the supermarket even if it is at a heavily discounted rate.

This sort of power may allow a firm to exploit its suppliers in the knowledge that the supplier has few options beyond selling to the sole buyer. This can mean that cheaper prices are passed on to the consumer, but only at the expense of the supplier of the goods.

There are some advantages of monopsony: lower prices are passed on to consumers, and quality might be better than if there was perfect competition in buying resources. Monopsony power might balance out monopoly power. For example, some 'DOC' wine-producing regions use their monopoly power to charge a high price, but supermarkets (monopsonists) can force them to supply at lower prices in order to make a high volume of sales.

Contestability

A **contestable market** is said to exist when it has low sunk costs and therefore low barriers to entry and exit. This may be because an industry does not have a dominant firm with high brand recognition, requiring large amounts to be spent on advertising (which is a sunk cost) in order to gain market share. This means that new firms can

Monopsony Where there is a sole buyer of a good. For example, the government is the sole buyer of defence equipment in the UK. Government can use this power to extract the best price for itself, often by reducing the producer surplus the selling firm receives. Firms can use these powers to exploit their suppliers and drive down prices.

Monopsony refers to buying power, not to selling power.

Can the competition authorities regard *any* action of monopsonies as illegal?

Contestable market A market with low sunk costs and therefore low barriers to entry. This sort of market is synonymous with 'hit and run' profits.

quickly enter an industry when they see supernormal profits being made and exploit these before leaving the industry again: for example, when prices fall. These are referred to as 'hit and run' profits.

A whole range of industries can be said to have become contestable in recent years. The airline industry is an obvious example, with the advent of low-cost airlines such as Ryanair and EasyJet. These airlines were able to lease aeroplanes and access smaller, regional airports, which had lower costs, and this enabled them to establish a foothold in the market. They did not spend significant amounts on advertising but were able to establish market share by offering a new product, thereby overcoming the brand recognition that the major flag carriers such as BA and Lufthansa had. It could be argued that now that Ryanair and EasyJet are so well established, the industry is much less contestable because new firms will not be able to enter the market and gain market share.

Signs of a high level of contestability (low barriers to entry and exit) are:

- low fixed costs, e.g. low levels of high-tech machinery required
- low sunk costs, e.g. minimal advertising on a national scale
- weak brand names/very few patents
- low potential profitability in the long run.

The signs of an uncontestable market are the reverse of the above, but you might also observe:

- strong oligopoly or market power of incumbent firms, e.g. limit pricing might be used to keep out possible entrants
- high levels of non-price competition, e.g. firms are trying to raise barriers to entry by increasing brand loyalty, perhaps by endorsing a sporting competition
- investigations by the CMA. Although the competition authorities might not take many actions against some industries, the frequency of their investigation can imply that other firms have found it difficult to compete. The energy markets are often being investigated, for example.

Exam tip

A highly contestable market has low barriers to entry or exit. Do not confuse it with a highly concentrated market, which tends to have high barriers.

Exam tip

You may be asked to consider industries that have become contestable in recent years, such as convenience stores, chewing gum and the pharmaceutical industry. All of these industries have traditionally had high barriers to entry but have recently seen a growth of new firms, perhaps due to new technical processes, which allow firms to enter the market cheaply, or the development of the internet as a low-cost means of advertising and retailing.

Knowledge check 22

What is the difference between a competitive market and a contestable one?

Summary

- There are four market structures that you need to know, in terms of selling: perfect competition, monopolistic competition, oligopoly and monopoly.
- In terms of buying, you need to know monopsony, a powerful or single buyer.
- Game theory is used to explain much of the behaviour of interdependent firms in an oligopoly. The most useful tool to explain this in an exam is a simple game theory matrix.

- Price discrimination occurs when the same good is sold at different prices in different markets. The model is used mainly in the context of monopoly and shows that the profit maximisation concept of $MC = MR$ can be extended to submarkets where the MR is different and therefore profits can be increased.
- A contestable market is a market with low or no barriers to entry or exit, where the threat of competition can change the behaviour of firms significantly.

Labour market

In this section the demand and supply of labour is considered. The demand for labour comes from firms and is a derived demand based on the demand for goods and services. The supply of labour is from households. The interaction of demand and supply will determine the wage rate that this labour receives. A number of factors will determine the level of wages paid, including the level of skills and the price elasticity of supply, i.e. the speed with which an employer may be able to recruit additional workers.

Demand for labour

The demand for labour is a derived demand, made by firms. As the demand for the firm's output increases then the demand for labour to produce this output also increases. Therefore in times when the economy is growing, the demand for labour increases and at the same time the level of employment in the economy increases. The opposite is also true, so that if the level of economic output were to decline, it would see a decrease in the demand for goods and services and therefore a decline in the demand for labour, resulting in unemployment.

As workers become more productive, the demand for labour increases and so does their ability to demand higher wages, as their marginal productivity increases.

Of course, firms can substitute labour for capital, so if capital becomes more expensive, firms will employ more labour, but also if labour were to become more expensive, the demand for capital would increase. In certain economies it is said that firms will specialise in capital-intensive processes because labour is highly skilled and expensive. This tends to be the case in the developed world, whereas in the developing world, where labour is abundant and lacking in skills, it is cheaper to employ workers than it is to automate a process.

> **Knowledge check 23**
>
> What factors determine the level of demand in different economies?

Supply of labour

The supply of labour will depend on a number of factors, which include the rewards for supplying labour: in other words, the wage rate (known as pecuniary benefits), the benefits associated with working in a certain place, such as the quality of the office, colleagues and general working environment (known as the non-pecuniary benefits), and the level of taxation or welfare provision.

These rewards will be determined by the level of skills and qualifications required from employees, and the ease of recruitment, which in turn may be determined by the working conditions and the relative importance of trade unions. Work is seen to be an inferior good, so it has a negative income elasticity of demand. Thus, as income rises initially, the supply of labour will increase, but after a certain level it will fall as workers substitute work with leisure.

Market failure

Market failure can result from geographical and occupational immobility of labour.

Geographical immobility

This occurs when people cannot relocate to another part of the country to take up job opportunities. This may be due to differentials in house prices or a desire not to relocate and break up the family. This can be a problem for people from other parts of the UK who want to relocate and work in and around London.

Occupational immobility

This is when workers are unable to change jobs or take up new opportunities due to a lack of skills or training. In the UK, as the economy has undergone structural changes, moving away from a manufacturing base to a service-based economy, many employees have found that their skills are no longer required and they do not possess the necessary skills for the new jobs in the economy.

Knowledge check 24

Are wages paid the only factor that determines the supply of labour?

Wage determination in competitive markets

The competitive market for labour works like the markets for the other factors of production, such as land and capital which were studied in Theme 1. The interaction of demand and supply creates the price for labour: in other words, the equilibrium wage rate.

If wages are too high then the supply of labour will be greater than the demand for labour: for example, at W_3 in Figure 25. This excess labour is known as unemployment. In a competitive market, workers will compete for the available employment opportunities and therefore will compete wages down to the equilibrium or market-clearing wage rate of W_e in Figure 25.

However, if the wages are too low, for example at W_2, then the demand for labour will be high, at Q_2, while the supply of labour will be low, at Q_1, resulting in a shortage of labour. Workers will not be willing to work at this wage rate as they are not being paid enough to compensate them for the opportunity cost associated with working. In order to hire more workers, the wage rate will have to increase to the market-clearing wage rate at W_e and therefore increase the rewards to workers for their time and efforts.

Exam tip

Wage determination can be examined in the context of the demand and supply for labour in a number of contexts: for example, the labour market for street sweepers, nurses, lawyers and doctors. You should be able to explain why there are differences in the salaries that each of these different workers receives in return for supplying their services.

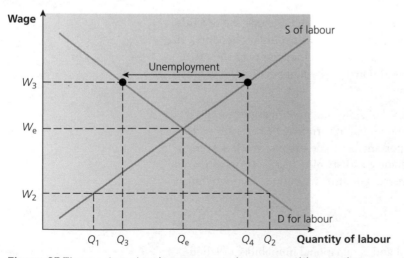

Figure 25 The market-clearing wage rate in a competitive market

In the UK, successive governments have invested significant time and money to try to reduce the level of youth unemployment, by increasing young people's skills and training. Schemes promising more apprenticeships and places at university are designed to reduce the levels of occupational immobility that exist, especially among the young.

In the period after the 2008 global economic crisis the UK saw a significant increase in unemployment, but also one of the fastest falls in unemployment of any OECD country post 2012. Some economists argue this was a consequence of the UK having a flexible labour market, which allows businesses to recruit workers on temporary, flexible or zero-hours contracts and dismiss them within two years with few consequences. However, other economists would argue that these types of contract are exploitative and do not allow employees to establish a pattern of prolonged employment.

Wage determination in non-competitive markets

The national minimum wage is a legally enforced minimum that firms must pay employees. In the UK that minimum wage was introduced in 1999.

In Figure 26 we can see that a minimum wage has been introduced at W_1. For a minimum wage to be effective it must be above the equilibrium wage rate of W_e. As a result of the introduction of the minimum wage, the supply of labour increases to Q_2 but at the same time the demand for labour falls to Q_1. This results in an excess supply of labour and therefore unemployment between Q_1 and Q_2.

In recent years firms, charities and commentators have placed increased importance on the 'living wage', which is higher than the minimum wage and is determined by the Living Wage Foundation. It has been adopted by a number of employers, including ITV, Barclays Bank and Transport for London, in place of the national minimum wage. In the budget of July 2015 the Chancellor of the Exchequer committed to the introduction of a National Living Wage, enforceable by law – specifically, a minimum wage of £9 per hour by 2020 for anyone over the age of 25.

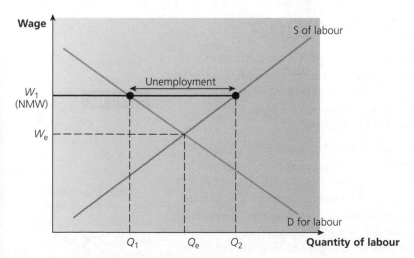

Figure 26 The national minimum wage

Knowledge check 25

Would an increase in productivity shift the demand curve for labour to the right and therefore allow higher wages to be paid?

Exam tip

Politicians argue as to whether or not the flexible labour market is exploitative and have reformed the labour market quite significantly in recent years. It is important that you are aware of recent changes, including changes to employment conditions such as zero-hours contracts and welfare reforms which may impact on people's desire to work.

Exam tip

You need to be able to give the arguments for and against the introduction of a minimum wage and understand its impact on employment and the standard of living.

Knowledge check 26

Does a rise in the national minimum wage cause unemployment?

Elasticity of demand and supply of labour

Elasticity of demand for labour refers to the responsiveness of demand to changes in the wage rate. If demand is said to be price (meaning 'wage', the price of labour) inelastic, then if wages were to increase, the impact on demand would be limited. This is typical in industries where workers are skilled and cannot be easily replaced with either cheaper workers or capital equipment. When the demand for labour is wage elastic, meanwhile, an increase in wages is likely to result in a large decrease in the demand for labour, with workers often being replaced by capital equipment.

The wage elasticity of demand for labour will depend on cost of labour relative to the overall cost of running the business, the time it takes to locate alternative manufacturing processes and the time period being referred to. In the short term it is usually hard to replace labour, so demand tends to be wage inelastic, but in the long run it can be replaced, for example with machines, so the demand for labour tends to be wage elastic.

Elasticity of supply of labour refers to the responsive of workers or potential workers to changes in the wage rate. If supply is said to be price (meaning 'wage', the price of labour) inelastic, then if wages were to increase, the impact on supply would be limited. This is typical in industries where workers take time to acquire skills or training and cannot easily enter the market.

If a particular job requires a number of years' training and specific skills, then the price or wage elasticity of supply is relatively inelastic, so as demand increases for that job – for example, if the government announces it wants an additional 2,000 surgeons – then wages will increase. However, in the long run additional training will mean that surgeons become relatively abundant, and so as wages increase there is a steady stream of people able to work at a high level of specialism in the medical profession, making supply relatively wage elastic in the long run. Clearly, in such instances, living in a global market will mean that the economy can recruit from abroad, using migration to increase the supply of workers, helping to plug the skills shortage and keep wages from increasing, as well as satisfying the increased demand.

Government intervention

Governments intervene in the working of businesses to maintain competition in markets. There are two major methods: competition policy (enforcing competition law, which prevents abuse of market dominance and actions that prevent competitiveness) and regulation (introducing direct controls on firms, such as price caps, where increasing competition does not solve market failure problems).

Competition policy is the means by which governments of countries and groups of countries seek to restore and maintain competition in markets, to ensure efficient working of markets and improved consumer welfare. The aim of competition policy is to ensure that any action that 'prevents, restricts or distorts competition' is blocked and that fair trading is enforced: that is, restrictive practices such as predatory pricing and collusion should be stamped out. The Competition and Markets Authority was established in April 2014, replacing the Competition Commission and the Office of Fair Trading.

Exam tip

Remember the formulas for price elasticity of demand and supply (Theme 1) and factors that determine whether the demand or supply of labour is wage elastic or inelastic.

Exam tip

The same determinants of price elasticity of demand and supply found in Theme 1 can be applied to the wage elasticity of demand and supply for labour.

Exam tip

You may be asked to consider competition policy in any economy, although the structures and systems used in the UK will transfer easily to the country you will be asked to consider.

Government intervention to control mergers

The minimum condition for investigation is if a **merger** of firms will result in a market share greater than 25% or if it meets the 'turnover test' of a combined turnover of £70 million or more. The Competition and Markets Authority determines whether a merger will impact adversely on competition. In other words, if the merger leads to a 'substantial lessening of competition', it is likely to be blocked. This market share may allow a firm to exhibit the characteristics of a monopoly and dominate the market. Since the Enterprise Act of 2002, there have been new powers for the competition authorities, and from 2012 the functions of the competition authorities were combined, so you must make sure that you keep up to date with developments. Remember, too, that the fact that a merger *may* be referred to the competition authorities does not mean that it *must* be, nor does it mean it will be stopped. There are important cases when a referral or block does not happen. An example is when the merger satisfies an obvious national interest: the merger may then take place regardless of the impact on competition. This was clearly the case in September 2008 when the government set aside the concerns of the competition authorities to allow the merger between Lloyds TSB and HBOS, despite the fact that it would leave the newly merged Lloyds Banking Group with more than 35% of the current account market.

> **Merger** The joining together of at least two firms to form one entity.

> **Exam tip**
>
> Make sure that you know about two or three recent decisions by the competition authorities. You are likely to be given an opportunity to discuss a case study from your own knowledge in the exam.

Government intervention to control monopolies

Monopoly power is not necessarily undesirable (see the table showing the costs and benefits of monopoly on pages 34–35), but the competition authorities aim to stop a firm abusing its dominant position. Any action such as collusion, acting as a cartel or deliberately preventing new entry of firms (such as through predatory pricing) is targeted when oligopolies try to increase their profits at the expense of customers or other non-colluding firms. Any attempt to fix prices is illegal in the UK, and even talking about prices with other firms is counted as collusion. Controlling suppliers or retail networks is also highly anti-competitive, and therefore vertical integration (see pages 8–9) is subject to careful scrutiny by the competition authorities. In 2011, for example, the nine supermarkets in the UK were found to be fixing the price of milk and cheese products – Tesco alone was fined £10 million.

> **Knowledge check 27**
>
> Almost all cases referred to the EU competition authorities are cleared. Does this mean their powers are not very effective?

Regulation is direct government control of firms, used when market forces are judged to be inadequate as a means of protecting consumer interests. Unlike in competition policy, the government tries to act as a **surrogate for competition** by making firms cut prices, or takes legal action: for example, forcing the sell-off of parts of BAA or introducing banking codes where it believes that in a free market the firms do not act in the best interests of all involved. If regulation is not followed, the firms can be fined or can lose their right to operate.

> **Exam tip**
>
> 'A surrogate for competition' is a useful expression: after privatisation, many of the firms continued to exist as **natural** monopolies: they were heavily regulated by independent watchdogs, which acted as if they were competing firms (by forcing prices down), until competition could replace regulation.

After privatisation of the state-owned monopolies such as British Telecom, British Gas and the electricity and water industries in the 1980s and early 1990s, the government appointed a regulator as a surrogate for competition to set price and maintain quality in the industries. Once in private ownership, these firms were answerable to shareholders, who wished to maximise their return on their investment in the form of greater profits. Since competition has been established in the telecoms, gas and electricity industries, there has been no need for regulation on the same scale as in the past, but the previously state-owned industries that are in possession of monopoly power (water and the railway sectors) still have their prices set by the regulator. Regulation includes the setting of price caps, performance targets or other sorts of monitoring of firms by the government, to ensure that firms do not abuse their market dominance.

Price regulation

Price capping is used to regulate several privatised **utilities** in the UK. The price cap is an upper limit set on the increase that the firms can add to their retail prices. It takes into account the level of inflation measured by the retail price index (RPI – a measure of inflation that you will have come across in Theme 2) and then takes account of possible efficiency gains or investment.

RPI – X

This takes the RPI and subtracts a factor X determined by the regulator. X represents the efficiency gains that the regulator has determined can reasonably be achieved by the firm in question.

RPI + K

This takes the RPI and allows the addition of the K factor, which accounts for the additional capital spending that a firm has agreed with the regulator is necessary. This is used by the water regulators to determine the price for each of the regional water companies. The K factor is different for each of the water companies, depending on how much they are required to spend to maintain and improve their quality of service. A similar system is used for train-operating companies.

The advantage of price capping is that it allows a firm to keep any profits it makes through bringing about greater efficiency gains than the regulator has calculated are reasonable. In addition, because the X and K factors are usually in place for a reasonable period, say five years, firms are able to plan ahead and know that they will not be unduly penalised for making further efficiency gains.

However, this method can be criticised. If the regulator underestimates the efficiency gains a firm can be expected to make, then firms can produce what appear to be excessive profits, although often these profits are used to invest in areas outside the regulator's remit and therefore generate even greater profits in the future. There have been suggestions in the past that the regulator and the regulated industry have built up a close relationship, resulting in the regulator being less strict on the firms under its control. This close relationship is referred to as **regulatory capture**.

Profit regulation

This method allows a firm to make a certain level of profit based on its capital stock before the remainder of the profit is taxed at 100%. Unlike the price-capping system, this means that there is no incentive to make efficiency gains that increase profits. Firms are not rewarded for their success; on the contrary, they are penalised for it and instead encouraged to make a limited profit. Any excess profit is therefore spent on additional capital to increase the level of capital stock and therefore allowable profit while increasing the level of efficiency. At the same time, firms are encouraged to overstate the value of their capital or embark on wasteful spending to ensure that they can increase the rate of return on their investment, in effect increasing their profits, and therefore profit regulation is being replaced by price or revenue caps in the USA.

Knowledge check 28

What is privatisation and why was it so important in the UK in the 1980s and 1990s?

Exam tip

A price cap is a form of regulation that sets a cap on the amount that certain firms can raise their prices. It is therefore the **maximum** price increase that the firm can impose on its customers and is usually based on the rate of inflation as measured by the RPI.

Knowledge check 29

What does X represent in the price cap formula RPI – X?

Performance standards and quality targets

The regulator can also set performance targets that it will then monitor. These may be based on improvements in the quality of service or reductions in the number of customer complaints. This may be supported by a system of fines, should the firm fail to meet the performance targets, or rewards, should the firm meet them. This has been used by the regulator to monitor the punctuality of trains in the UK and to help determine future price increases. Penalties can be attached to the targets so that consumers derive the benefit if customer service falls below a minimum standard.

Other regulation

Controls in response to the credit crisis

The banking industry is now subject to heavy regulation in terms of the amounts it can lend and the risks it can take. Although several major UK banks were partially nationalised, those that were not (such as Barclays) are still subject to new, tougher regulations.

Controls from outside the UK

Direct controls from the EU take precedence over UK rules – for example, limits on carbon emissions or employment rules – and decisions by other bodies, such as the World Trade Organization (WTO), would tend to override business decisions in the UK.

Government intervention to promote contestability

Governments the world over seek to promote contestability in markets in order to give consumers the benefit of greater choice, innovation and competition. Governments can do this through reductions in barriers to entry – a perfectly contestable market in theory having no barriers to entry – and reductions in restrictive practices, both of which will increase the scope for new firms to enter the market.

Incumbent firms will often use their position, perhaps in the form of various pricing strategies and legal barriers that they may possess, such as patents or access to a particular technology, to ensure that the market does not become contestable. However, regulators will consider whether the behaviour of the incumbent – for example, by restricting the supply of raw materials, entering into exclusive agreements or engaging in anti-competitive pricing – restricts freedom of entry, and the regulators may then intervene to open up markets.

In addition, the government will seek to promote start-up businesses as these firms are able to establish themselves as potential challengers to existing operators, especially if they are able to identify a particular segment of the market that has not previously been exploited.

Privatisation, competitive tendering and deregulation

Privatisation is the process by which the government transfers the ownership of a state-owned enterprise from the public sector to the private sector. A recent example has been the sale of Royal Mail into the private sector. Now with shareholders to satisfy, the newly privatised firm will seek to maximise profits and therefore to make significant increases in sales and efficiencies, thus reducing costs.

Knowledge check 30

What kind of regulation is it when train-operating firms are forced to refund passengers if their train is more than an hour late?

When it is possible, these firms will be allowed to compete with other firms, such as in the case of the telecommunications industry where consumers have a choice whether or not to use BT, the previous state monopoly, or one of the competitors in the market. Where it is not possible to create competition, the state will regulate the industry, as discussed on pages 43–45.

Some activities that were previously undertaken by the government are now performed by the private sector on behalf of the government, in jobs that have been contracted out. These include the movement of prisoners, which is subcontracted to the private sector, and hospital catering and cleaning. The process by which these contracts are won is known as **competitive tendering** and often results in the cheapest, most cost-effective bid winning. However, as firms compete to lower their bids and therefore charge the government less for the contract, savings and therefore sacrifices in quality may have to be made.

Finally, certain markets, such as the bus sector, have been opened to competition through the deregulation of the market. This process, in which barriers to entry are removed, means that any firm, within reason, can set up a company to operate in a market, thereby creating competition, reducing prices, increasing quality and thus benefiting the consumer.

Competitive tendering
The process by which a number of private-sector firms compete to win the right to perform a task on behalf of the government. They will charge the government for the particular task and seek to make a profit.

Government intervention to protect suppliers and employees

The government will intervene in the ways described, through the Competition and Markets Authority as well as through legislation and the creation of competition, to increase competition and therefore reduce the power of monopsonists. This will help protect suppliers who would otherwise be vulnerable to exploitation by the monopsonist. For example, the Competition and Markets Authority is investigating supermarkets to determine whether or not they are exploiting their market dominance and extracting unfair prices from their suppliers. They could be fined if they have behaved in a way that is anti-competitive, although this is scant compensation for those suppliers that may have gone out of business in the interim.

Impact of government intervention

As already discussed, the government, through the regulator, can break up and fine firms as well as block mergers and jail executives who embark on anti-competitive practices. In such instances the government will hope to increase competition and therefore reduce prices, as well as increase quality and innovation within markets.

In certain instances a firm may be prevented from merging with another because it will be seen to reduce competition, despite the fact they may actually cease to trade because of this restriction, especially if they face competition from abroad. Increasingly, local regulators play only a small part in deciding the fate of a business as the role of international regulators takes on added importance because of globalisation and the interconnectedness of markets.

Limits to government intervention

Government actions can also result in government failure: in other words, the actions of the government actually move the industry away from the socially optimal level of output that the government was trying to achieve.

In many cases regulators have years of experience in the industry that they are now expected to regulate, this often being the best way to identify people who can regulate an industry. In some instances the regulator may also experience regulatory capture as a result and therefore be seen to reduce the scope of penalties applied to firms or even turn a blind eye to their actions.

Firms will closely guard much of their data surrounding costs, innovations, pricing strategies and employment, especially where this may be commercially sensitive, and therefore make it very difficult for the regulator to form a complete picture of the business. In some cases the firm will possess significantly more information than the regulator and therefore be in a strong position to prevent competition. This asymmetric information, where one party has access to more information than another, means that the regulator is unable to fulfil its duties.

Summary

- Competition policy is used to prevent the abuse of market power and to prevent acts that do not allow fair competition, such as a merger or an act of collusion.
- A merger or acquisition may be referred to the competition authorities to prevent large monopolies forming.
- The competition authorities investigate a wide range of actions by firms that might lessen competition and there have been significant powers to ensure competition exists among firms since the 2002 Enterprise Act.
- Regulation is a form of direct control or set of rules for private firms.
- *RPI – X* is a price-control method for regulating some privatised utilities, and *K* can be added to allow for increases in investment. There are advantages of this method of regulation, especially when compared with the US rate of return method, but there are also some significant drawbacks.
- Privatisation – the sale of state-owned assets into the private sector – includes deregulation of markets and competitive tendering.
- Regulators may experience regulatory capture or asymmetric information, which in turn reduces their ability to do their job of regulating a market.

Questions & Answers

Exam format

A-level Paper 1 comprises 35% of the weighting for the A-level examination. The time allowed is 2 hours. This paper will include some Theme 1 concepts and some Theme 3 concepts. You should therefore use your Theme 1 and Theme 3 books together in your preparation for Paper 1, but the paper is not fully synoptic, in that you would not be expected to use material from Themes 2 or 4 (macroeconomics). There are three sections, with A worth 25 marks, B worth 50 marks and C (the essay section) worth 25 marks, making a total of 100 marks. You will have choice on Section C only and this will be a choice from two microeconomic essays.

Paper 3 of the A-level covers content from all four themes. You will need to make connections between the content of this guide and that of the other three themes, so you should use all four Student Guides to gain a firm understanding of the economics specification as a whole. It is a 2-hour exam with two sections equally weighted at 50 marks each. In each of Sections A and B there are compulsory questions a) to c) and an optional essay d) or e), so you have to answer a total of six shorter questions and write two essays. Paper 3 is the only fully synoptic paper, meaning that the questions can be drawn from any part of Themes 1 to 4.

The following exam-type questions are largely based on Theme 3, although some synoptic elements have been included because in your second year of economics you must become skilled in using other parts of the course in your answers. Note that the questions here have not been accredited by Edexcel and the author has no knowledge of the style or content of future questions apart from the two sets of sample assessment materials that are available online at bit.ly/1RBdxXY.

All Edexcel data-response questions are based on real-life examples. In recent years the questions have considered the banking, airline, foods, utilities, car, pharmaceuticals and supermarket industries. It is therefore worth reading a quality newspaper or business website to develop a good idea of the major industrial changes, and listening to analytical programmes on the radio, such as the BBC's *The Bottom Line*. Often having this kind of background understanding, although not essential, will give you a head-start over other candidates, and you will have the opportunity to talk about your own knowledge of microeconomics.

How to use the data and extract

When examiners write the question papers, they spend hours trying to ensure that every paragraph, piece of data and graph they include is helpful in answering the question set. It is vital, therefore, that you use the data and extract to help you answer the questions. It may be that the information is included as background or it may give you a steer as to the sort of answers the examiners are expecting. If the instructions in the question paper direct you to use the information (for instance, by saying *'with reference to Extract A…'*), it is worth your while doing so, as there are certainly some marks reserved for this. However, avoid quoting too much from the data or extract (unless it is directly relevant to the answer that you are giving) as this will just waste valuable time.

Analysing data

Data should be handled in a particular way. It is important that you try to manipulate it to help you answer the question. For example, you may encounter questions asking you to *'Assess the trend that the data show'*, *'Calculate the percentage change'* or *'Calculate the market share of a firm'* from the data given to you. In these cases, avoid analysing the data by considering what has happened year by year. It is better to look at the overall picture and then draw conclusions.

Make sure you understand the data and charts fully. What does each axis mean? Is this a percentage increase or is the subject matter measured in thousands or millions? Always check whether the data show a firm's sales *falling* or *rising less quickly*. Be willing to use the data, calculate percentage changes and work out the trend over the time frame described.

Be willing to challenge the data. What is the source? Could it be biased? Is it too short a period of time to gain a definitive understanding of the position the business or industry faces? What more information would you like to see to give you a better understanding of the firm or industry?

Evaluation

The higher marked parts of each question will contain evaluation. The command words for evaluation are 'assess', 'discuss', 'examine', 'to what extent' and 'evaluate'. Be willing to use the various cases you have read about to illustrate the points you are making and demonstrate the counter-arguments. You may even be able to go beyond the confines of the extract, using application from your own knowledge.

How to evaluate

There are many ways to evaluate, but the key element is to offer critical distance, or a different viewpoint from the one already explained. You can consider any of the five points made here, as long as they are adapted to suit the context of the question, or use others that you will have come across in your reading.

- **Time.** Consider the time frame being looked at. Are the data over 1 year? Could there be more information? Do the data give you only a brief snapshot? Also contrast the short-run impact of any changes you discuss with the long-run impact. Consider how long it will take for something to happen – will it take a few months for an airline to expand operations or will it take some years? This can also be related to the price elasticity of supply: in other words, how easily the firm is going to be able to react to a change in the price of the good and increase supply.
- **Size of change.** You should always consider the magnitude of any change, calculate the percentage change and then draw conclusions as to whether this is significant. For example, profits of £500 million may appear a lot, but when set against sales of £10 billion, in fact they represent only 5% of all sales and may not be as significant. Or consider how much a firm is willing to spend on advertising, or research and development; if this is a small percentage of overall sales, it may

make very little impact on the overall demand of the good. Or, when looking at the penalties that a government or regulator may impose for restrictive practices, if these represent a small proportion of overall profits or revenues, perhaps the firms will feel able to collude or price fix.

- **Likelihood.** Consider how likely something is to happen. For example, how likely is the government to renationalise the railway industry? There may be other factors to consider, such as the cost of nationalisation or government failure, how will the competition authorities react, and if found to be illegal, what will be the impact of the fine?

- **Wider impact.** Consider what the effect will be on the industry or the economy. How might other firms react? For example, if a firm lowers prices to try to gain an increased share of the market, might this result in a price war? Or if a firm embarks on an ambitious advertising policy, will this only encourage other firms to do much the same? Or instead would it benefit all parties to collude, despite this being illegal?

- **Prioritisation of factors.** One of the easiest ways to evaluate is to rank in order of significance the points made – in other words, which of the points made in the answer is most important and is going to have the greatest effect? This will need to be justified, but it may be quite simple to do this. For example, when answering a question about pricing and non-pricing strategies that a firm might follow to increase demand, a candidate could evaluate the effectiveness of the two strategies, concluding that one is more likely to work because it is affordable, or the economic environment allows it to be implemented easily.

Evaluation is a skill and, like all skills, it can be developed through practice. As you read an article or watch a news item, ask yourself these questions and discuss them with others.

■ Paper 1

Multiple-choice and short answer questions

This part of the book contains eight multiple-choice and short answer questions. It is designed to be a key learning, revision and exam preparation resource. You should use these questions to reinforce your understanding of the specification subject matter and as practice for completing work under test conditions.

The multiple-choice and short answer questions are similar in structure and style to the Paper 1 examination. However, in the examination each question is placed on a separate page with lines for your answer, in order to provide room for diagrams and calculations.

A maximum of 5 marks can be scored for each short answer, Section A, A-level question. In this book, correct answers are given at the end of the section, together with mark schemes indicating how explanation marks may be awarded. The sets of short answer questions cover different topics in the specification. You are strongly advised to attempt the topic-based questions only when you have completed your revision for a topic.

In the examination, the multiple-choice questions will be computer marked, so you will need to mark the answer by the key that you choose. If you change your mind you must mark clearly that the answer you no longer want is rejected (with a cross-through) or it will look as if you have chosen two answers and the computer will automatically mark this as wrong. For the other questions there are lines provided, with at least two lines for every mark allocated. Do not feel you have to use all of the space provided – the intention is to allow for large handwriting and crossings out, rather than for everyone to fill every line. Always check with the mark scheme after you have completed the questions, either as you go along or at the end.

The multiple-choice questions are always worth 1 mark only. The value of the other questions (as outlined on the accredited specimen questions) is as follows:

- Calculate (2 or 4 marks)
- Explain (2 or 4 marks)
- Draw/illustrate (4 marks)

Question 1 Costs and revenues

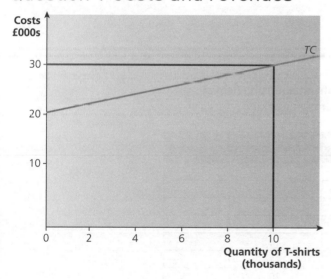

(a) The diagram shows the total cost for Jamie, a manufacturer of T-shirts. At an output of 10 000, the average variable cost is:

A £30 000

B £10 000

C £1

D £3

(1 mark)

ℯ There are many practice questions similar to this on the old 6EC03 papers on the Edexcel website. Practice questions are extremely valuable for this kind of question and cannot change significantly over time.

(b) Jamie finds that by lowering the price of the T-shirts from £5.50 to £5.00, annual sales rise from 10 000 to 11 000. Calculate the change in the marginal revenue.

(2 marks)

(e) Remember to show your working. Both of the marks are for the calculation and not the definitions, although using a definition will make your calculations easier to follow.

(c) Jamie's products face a downward-sloping demand curve. Using the concept of price elasticity of demand, explain the effect on total revenue if she cuts the price below £5.

(2 marks)

(e) A downward-sloping demand curve means that the firm is not in perfect competition (i.e. a price taker). You cannot assume, however, that it is a monopoly, because it could be in monopolistic competition, oligopoly or monopoly. The key thing is that the MR is also downward sloping and falls at twice the rate of the demand curve.

Question 2 Motives of the firm

(a) Samwei is a firm producing smartphones. It has the objective of sales maximisation. It will seek to set:

A   Marginal cost equal to marginal revenue.

B   Marginal cost equal to average revenue.

C   Marginal revenue equal to zero.

D   Average revenue equal to average cost.

(1 mark)

(b) The table shows the costs and revenues for a profit-maximising firm at equilibrium. The final column is left blank for your own working.

Output per week	Total revenue (£000s)	Marginal revenue (£000s)	Total cost (£000s)	Marginal cost (£000s)	
0	0	–	10	–	
1	20	20	14	4	
2	38	18	19	5	
3	54	16	28	9	
4	68	14	42	14	
5	80	12	63	21	
6	90	10	93	30	

Calculate the range of output at which the firm will operate and the level of profit that it will make.

(2 marks)

(c) Another smartphone producer is making a loss. Explain why the smartphone firm might continue in business despite making a loss.

(2 marks)

Question 3 Theory of the firm: perfect competition

(a) Which of the following markets is closest to the model of perfect competition?

A   Retail banks

B   Fresh apples

C   Car manufacturing

D   Rail travel

(1 mark)

(b) The figure below shows a firm in perfect competition making a loss. Annotate the diagram to show the changes in the long run. (2 marks)

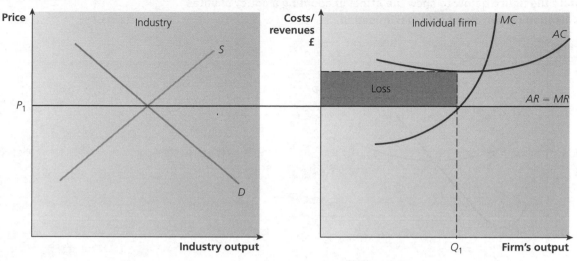

(c) Explain why firms that remain in a perfectly competitive industry when other firms leave will see their output increase. (2 marks)

ⓔ You can find an excellent video explanation of this on pajholden's YouTube channel, entitled 'Perfect competition'.

Question 4 Theory of the firm: monopolistic competition

(a) A monopolistically competitive firm operating in the long run will:

   A Be allocatively but not productively efficient.

   B Be both allocatively and productively efficient.

   C Be productively but not allocatively efficient.

   D Be neither productively nor allocatively efficient. (1 mark)

(b) Draw a diagram to show the long-run monopolistic competition equilibrium. (2 marks)

(c) Explain why only normal profit exists for a firm under monopolistic competition in the long run. (2 marks)

Question 5 Theory of the firm: oligopoly

(a) A manufacturer of chocolate bars may want to engage in non-price competition rather than price competition when selling its product because:

   A It is possible to create brand loyalty for chocolate bars.

   B Chocolate bars are price elastic in demand.

   C The marginal revenue and price of chocolates are the same.

   D Chocolate-producing firms may cut prices if other firms do. (1 mark)

(b) Using a model of oligopoly, explain interdependence between firms. (4 marks)

Question 6 Theory of the firm: monopoly

(a) Annotate the figure below to show the effect of adopting a policy of sales maximisation rather than profit maximisation. *(2 marks)*

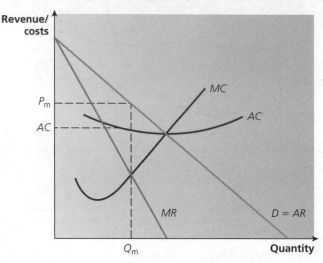

(b) Explain one reason why a firm operating under oligopoly may decide to pursue a goal that is not profit maximisation. *(2 marks)*

(c) C2 is a monopoly manufacturer of high-quality rugby trophies and operates at a profit-maximising level of output. Which of the following must be true?

  A Marginal revenue is negative.

  B Demand is relatively or perfectly price elastic.

  C Raising output will reduce the manufacturer's total revenue.

  D Demand is relatively or perfectly price inelastic. *(1 mark)*

Question 7 Labour market

(a) 'A private dentist practice (firm) increased its prices by 10% in 2015. Over the following year the number of treatments completed fell by 2%. The government has to subsidise the dentist industry as many patients do not pay for their own dental treatment directly.'

With reference to the context provided, calculate the price elasticity of demand for the dentist practice. You are advised to show your working. *(2 marks)*

(b) Which of the following is a likely reason for the value of the price elasticity of demand that you have calculated?

  A There are many other dentists offering similar services in the area.

  B Dental treatment is a public good.

  C The cost of dental treatment is a large proportion of potential customers' income.

  D Healthcare is seen as an essential part of spending for many customers. *(1 marks)*

(c) Explain one reason why dentists might be paid more than dental nurses. *(2 marks)*

ⓔ Remember to consider both the demand for and the supply of labour.

Question 8 Government intervention (competition policy)

(a) In 2015, four major British banks were found guilty of price fixing in the setting of the interbank interest rates, the LIBOR. Explain what is meant by 'price fixing'. (2 marks)

(b) The most likely reasons that the Competition and Markets Authority is likely to intervene in such cases is to bring into effect:

A A rise in shareholder value.

B An increase in consumer welfare.

C An increase in market concentration.

D Weaker contestability. (1 mark)

(c) The diagram below shows the costs and revenues for a bank before regulation.

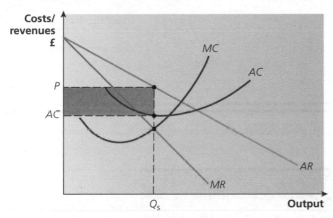

Annotate the diagram to show the likely effect on consumers resulting from an increase in competition between banks. (2 marks)

Answers to multiple-choice and short answer questions

Question 1 Costs and revenues

(a) Correct answer C.

ⓔ Total costs are £30 000. Fixed costs are £20 000 – remember, at an output of 0, the only costs that the firm incurs are fixed costs. Therefore, variable costs are £10 000, so average variable costs are £1 (£10 000/output of 10 000). (1/1 mark)

(b) There is no change.

ⓔ Marginal revenue is the change in total revenue from one more unit sold. Total revenue before the price cut is £550 000 × 10 = £5 500 000. This first stage in the calculation scores 1 mark. Total revenue after the price cut is £500 000 × 11 = £5 500 000. As a result, there has been no change in the total revenue and therefore no change in the marginal revenue of the business. This second stage in the calculation scores the second mark. Note that there is no mark for the definition itself, but this is very helpful for your reasoning and you are advised to state the definition, albeit briefly, at the start of any answer.

The correct answer is given but no working is shown. This is a very unwise policy and you should show every stage in your reasoning in case you make a small error and fail to gain full marks.

(2/2 marks)

(c) At £5 the *PED* is −1 or unitary. At any price below £5 the elasticity will be between −1 and 0. This is because the demand curve becomes less elastic as price falls/output rises. From this we can see that the marginal revenue will be less than 0 and the firm will make less revenue if it cuts its price. No rational firm would operate where the demand is inelastic.

e An excellent answer.

(2/2 marks)

Question 2 Motives of the firm

(a) Correct answer D.

e *AC = AR* Sales maximisation occurs where average revenue equals average cost.

(1/1 mark)

(b) See final column.

Output per week	Total revenue (£000s)	Marginal revenue (£000s)	Total cost (£000s)	Marginal cost (£000s)	Total profit (£000s)
0	0	–	10	–	−10
1	20	20	14	4	6
2	38	18	19	5	19
3	54	16	28	9	26
4	68	14	42	14	26
5	80	12	63	21	17
6	90	10	93	30	−3

The firm will operate between 3 and 4 units and the profit will be £26 000.

e This can be calculated using *TR − TC* and finding the maximum points (£26 000) or by using *MC = MR* (at £14 000).

(2/2 marks)

(c) If the firm covers its variable costs it might stay in business in order to make a contribution to fixed costs. This can be shown on a diagram:

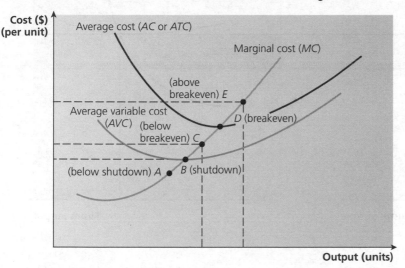

The shutdown point is point *B*: as long as a firm covers its average variable costs (*AVC*), it will continue to operate in the short run, even if it is making a loss, because it is making a contribution to fixed costs.

e The points that the firm must cover variable costs (1) and still carry on in business making a contribution (1) earn the full marks. The diagram would certainly be worth a third mark if it were required; however, it would be wise to add the contribution area – that is, the area showing the amount that the fixed costs are reduced by when the variable costs have been covered (see page 28).   (2/2 marks)

Question 3 Theory of the firm: perfect competition

(a) Correct answer B.

e Apples are often fairly similar, meaning they take the market-determined price; they use the same standard sizes, meaning they are to an extent homogeneous; the barriers to entry are relatively low and there are many apple growers on the global market. While this does not correlate exactly to the characteristics of perfect competition, it bears a close resemblance.

Banking and car manufacturing are dominated by a few firms and are best described as oligopolies. Rail travel is in a market to some extent characterised by natural monopoly.   (1/1 mark)

(b) The shutdown point shown in the figure below is for a perfectly competitive firm; however, the principle remains the same. As long as a firm covers its average variable costs, it will continue to operate in the short run, even if it is making a loss, because it is making a contribution to fixed costs.

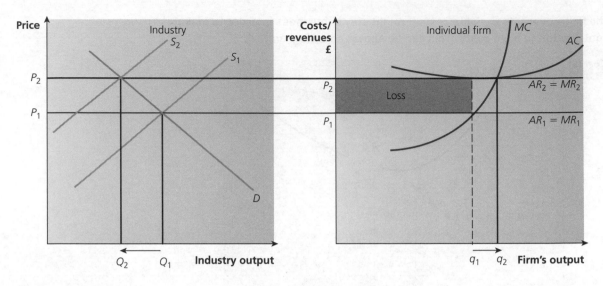

e

(2/2 marks)

(c) This is because prices rise for the firms left in the industry (1 mark), so they expand output to restore $MC = MR$, as shown in the right-hand panel of my diagram (1 mark).

e A model answer.

(2/2 marks)

Question 4 Theory of the firm: monopolistic competition

(a) Correct answer D.

e Productive efficiency occurs at the lowest point on the average cost curve. Allocative efficiency occurs at $P = MC$. In Figure 18, it is clear that neither of these occurs when the firm is profit maximising.

(1/1 mark)

(b)

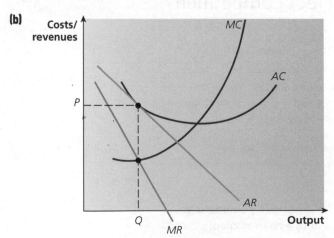

e In monopolistic competition, firms face low barriers to entry. Other firms will see supernormal profits being made in the short run and enter the industry, competing away these profits. Therefore, in the long run, monopolistically competitive firms will make only normal profits. At the profit-maximising level of output, $MC = MR$ and therefore the firm cannot be allocatively efficient $(P \neq MC)$. Accurate annotation. (2/2 marks)

(c) **Monopolistically competitive firms can make supernormal profits only in the short run because the low barriers to entry ensure any supernormal profits are competed away by new firms entering the industry. They are attracted by the profits and will continue to enter until the profits are gone – it is as if there is 'money on the table' and firms can continue to enter until it is all gone.**

ⓔ This scores well by describing barriers to entry and showing what happens to normal profit as firms compete it away. Another way to earn a mark would have been to define normal profit, but this is not required in the question. The mark scheme will not penalise you if you do not define something, unless it is specifically required in the question. (2/2 marks)

Question 5 Theory of the firm: oligopoly

(a) **Correct answer D.**

ⓔ One of the characteristics of an oligopoly is that only a few firms dominate the market. Therefore, in an oligopoly, firms are more likely to collude and fix prices to avoid price wars. (1/1 marks)

(b) **In an oligopoly, firms produce similar products, which ensures that the firms are interdependent. If a firm raises the price of its chocolate, few suppliers will follow, so revenue will fall. Equally, if the manufacturer lowers prices, others will do so and a price war will result, ensuring that total revenue falls. Therefore, oligopolists will aim to avoid price changes and create brand loyalty through non-price competition, such as advertising or changes in packaging.**

ⓔ A good analytical explanation of the kinked demand theory, or the payoff matrix, although not spelled out in these terms. The analysis is clear. (4/4 marks)

Alternative answer:

(b) **Oligopoly is a market structure where a few firms dominate the industry. One way to explain this is using the kinked demand curve. When a firm raises its price then other firms do not react so demand is relatively elastic, but when it cuts price all the other firms will do likewise and the demand will be relatively inelastic. There is an asymmetric reaction.**

ⓔ This is a good answer, although there is no analysis mark so it earns 3 out of 4. To get the final mark, it needs an explicit analysis of interdependence – that is, that the action of one firm is based on the action of another – and the answer should discuss the effects of this asymmetry, e.g. that the prices are sticky and the firm will tend to use non-price competition. Alternatively, there might be a fuller analytical response using a diagram (the kinked demand curve) or a payoff matrix. (3/4 marks)

Question 6 Theory of the firm: monopoly

(a)

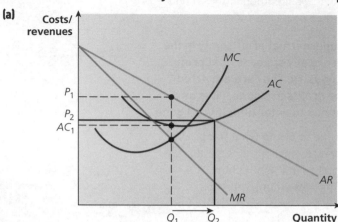

e 2 marks awarded for the point $AC = AR$ (1) and the new lower price/higher output (1).   (2/2 marks)

(b) The problem with profit maximisation $MC = MR$ is that high prices and profits might attract the attention of the competition authorities. By charging a lower price the firm is less likely to be observed and regulated, and the process of being examined, as well as the fines that might follow, could be very damaging to the firm's owners and for its reputation. There are many other goals the firm might pursue, for example revenue maximisation.

e The answer starts out perfectly in outlining the problems of profit maximising, but needs to show why the chosen alternative is better!   (1/2 marks)

(c) Correct answer B.

e This must be true because marginal costs by definition can never be negative – the least they can be is zero, and that is where the firm faces no variable costs, only fixed costs. For the equilibrium $MC = MR$ to hold, therefore, the value of MR must also be positive (or zero) and this occurs where the price elasticity of demand is relatively elastic (see page 15).   (1/1 mark)

Question 7 Labour market

(a) 0.2

e This is the correct answer using the formula % change in quantity demanded divided by % change in price, but it would be wise to write down this formula in case some of your working goes wrong.   (2/2 marks)

(b) Answer D.

e The context is healthcare, and for most customers there are not likely to be many alternatives to one particular dentist practice. Although prices might rise, many customers will continue to pay, and will have to make compromises in other areas of their family spending, or try to earn more rather than cut down significantly on the quantity of dental care received.   (1/1 mark)

(c) Dentists have more years of training and need much more skill than nurses, and it is very hard to get onto a course to learn to be a dentist. This reduces the supply of dentists relative to nurses, because although nurses now also need to have a degree, they do not need to get such high grades and pass the same high bars to get through a degree. It also takes almost twice as long to become a dentist, which has an opportunity cost because the students don't earn any money while they are training, and even though the NHS might pay the course fees, the dental student still has to find somewhere to live and pay for living costs. So the supply of labour is much limited than that for nurses.

e This answer would be much improved by considering also the demand for labour, which might reflect on the inelastic nature of demand for dentists, and the fact that the employer does not have cheap alternatives when employing dentists. A diagram could illustrate the relative demand and supply curves very effectively, with wage on the vertical axis.

(1/2 marks)

Question 8 Government intervention (competition policy)

(a) Price fixing is a form of collusive behaviour where firms raise prices knowing that other firms are unlikely to undercut them. Firms collude or act together to keep prices higher than they would have been without the collusion. It is illegal.

e This explains that prices are higher than they would be in competitive markets (1) and that it is collusion (1).

(2/2 marks)

(b) Correct answer B.

e The Competition and Markets Authority will intervene if it feels that it would result in an improvement in competition and hence consumer welfare.

(1/1 mark)

(c)

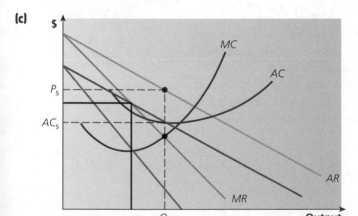

e This earns just 1 out of 2 marks because the new curves are not labelled and the new profit area (smaller) is not indicated. The answer could also have been valid by showing an increase in costs, but it would have to be clear which costs rise, fixed or variable.

(1/2 marks)

■ Paper 1 and Paper 3

Data-response questions

The data-response questions in this book resemble those in Section B of Paper 1 of the A-level examination and a selection of the first three questions in Sections A and B of Paper 3. In Paper 1 there will be *five* parts, adding up to a total of 50 marks (5, 8, 10, 12, 15), as well as the 25-mark essay (choice from two), and in Paper 3 there will be 5-, 8-, 12- and 15-mark questions, as well as the 25-mark essay (choice from two). All of these longer response questions have the emphasis on evaluation except for the first 5-mark question, where the emphasis is on data use. Ensure you read the material and try to use diagrams wherever possible to highlight your understanding of microeconomics.

As you will see in the sample assessment materials provided by Edexcel, there is no prescribed order of the questions, although the mark bases and marking structure will be unchanged for each question. The only question that does **not** require evaluation is the 5-mark question on Papers 1, 2 and 3. You must be very careful to remember that the 8-mark question does require evaluation, which is worth 2 marks.

There is a 'levels-based' approach to marking the data-response and open-extended questions, particularly those with a high mark tariff. This enables a variety of approaches in student answers to be valid rather than solely requiring specific points that are stated on the mark scheme. It means the examiner makes an initial assessment of the quality of an answer and places it at a level ranging from 1 to 4 (2 or 3 levels for a lower mark-based question). The examiner's judgement is then refined to award a more precise mark within that level. It is recommended that you refer to the levels descriptors provided at the end of the longer questions in the sample assessment materials for Economics on the Edexcel website: http://bit.ly/1HYjSKS

In addition, a levels-based mark scheme is often broken down into two further parts: the first focuses on 'knowledge, application and analysis' marks and the second relates to 'evaluation'. The command words used for evaluation questions are: *examine*, *evaluate*, *assess*, *discuss*, and *to what extent*. Any of these words in the question indicate that you should demonstrate some critical understanding of the issues being discussed. For A-level Paper 1 the following are the only command words that will be used:

- Explain/calculate (5 marks)
- Examine (8 marks)
- Assess (10 marks)
- Discuss (12 and 15 marks)
- Evaluate/to what extent (25 marks)

Paper 3, like Papers 1 and 2, is also 2 hours and is marked out of 100. There are two sections based on broad areas of the four themes, and while you would not expect both to be on the same area, there is no micro/macro split and you will need all four themes for both Section A and Section B of the paper. You might expect one section to be on a single domestic economy, one on international trade between economies, or one on developing economies, although this split is just an example. You will be given a large amount of data, taking the form of graphs and extracts, and you must spend some time reading the data carefully.

On Paper 3, the mark allocations are 5, 8, 12 and 25 in both Sections A and B. The 25-mark question involves a choice between two options.

- **Section A** Using data, explain (5 marks) × 1
  - Examine (8 marks) × 1
  - Discuss (12 marks) × 1
  - Evaluate/to what extent (25 marks): choose 1 from 2
- **Section B** Using data, explain (5 marks) × 1
  - Examine (8 marks) × 1
  - Discuss (12 marks) × 1
  - Evaluate/to what extent (25 marks): choose 1 from 2

Question 1 Royal Mail privatisation

ⓔ Note that Section B always starts on Question 6 in Paper 1 but for clarity in this book the questions are numbered from 1.

Extract 1 Department for Business succeeds in achieving its key objectives in the privatisation of Royal Mail

The government in 2014 welcomed the National Audit Office's (NAO) finding that the Department for Business succeeded in achieving its key objectives in the privatisation of Royal Mail. The NAO found that Royal Mail is now more likely to be able to operate the universal postal service without taxpayer support, sustaining the universally-priced, 6-days-a-week service required by law. Privatisation has reduced the risk to taxpayers. Royal Mail is now a profitable business with much improved cash flow, following government action and reforms.

A senior minister said: 'The National Audit Office's main finding is that we achieved what we set out to do. We secured the future of the universal postal service through a successful sale of a majority stake in Royal Mail, predominantly to responsible long term investors.

'Achieving the highest price possible at any cost and whatever the risk was never the aim of the sale. The report concludes there was a real risk of a failed sale attached to pushing the price too high. And a failed sale would have been the worst outcome for taxpayers, risking the vital 6 day a week service that customers and businesses around the country rely on.' The sale price for Royal Mail shares was set after a thorough process of engagement with more than 500 institutions, taking into account the company's industrial relations, market conditions at the time and professional assessment of Royal Mail's market value. The sale is standard market practice and is open, transparent, and allowed the government to offer the public the opportunity to buy shares.

By retaining a 30% stake in the business the government made sure taxpayers have benefited from dividend payments and will continue to benefit from share price rises after the sale.

Findings of the NAO report include:
- the government was right to place little reliance on the estimated potential valuations submitted by banks which were pitching to be part of the syndicate handling the sale
- the taxpayers' remaining 30% stake has appreciated in value and is worth more than £1.5 billion at current trading prices
- the government's estimate of the value of Royal Mail if retained in public ownership was less than £1 billion, compared with the nearly £2 billion raised from the sale of a majority stake
- it was right to appoint expert advisers, while the fees paid to the advisers were low compared with the market average and with government precedents.

The government published its objectives for the sale in April 2013, which were to sustain the universal service for the benefit of all users

→

Questions & Answers

(a) With reference to the data provided, explain what is meant by privatisation. (5 marks)

ⓔ For the 5-mark initial question, there are 2 marks for knowledge/application and 3 for analysis. You could give two brief points or one point with more detail. While it might help if you have studied the industry in advance, in terms of facility in answering the questions no prior knowledge of any specific industry is expected and you will find all that you need to know in the data provided.

(b) Using the data in Extract 1 and an appropriate diagram, assess reasons why Royal Mail is now 'a profitable business'. (10 marks)

ⓔ As with the old exam questions on 6EC03, it is very common to be asked for a diagram on the markets and business behaviour paper. You would expect to draw *AR* and *MR* shifting to the right, or a fall in *AC* and *MC* (if variable costs change) or a fall in *AC* (if a fixed cost changes).

(c) Discuss pricing and non-pricing strategies that Royal Mail could adopt to improve profitability. (12 marks)

ⓔ At A-level there must be scope for stretch and challenge and we therefore do not specify how many points are required in many cases. A safe course is to give at least one pricing and one non-pricing strategy, and no more than three in total, because if more than four factors are offered for a 12-mark question, only the best three are likely to be awarded marks.

For pricing strategies, make sure that you consider changes in price, based on economic rationale. Examples include revenue maximisation, output maximisation, limit pricing and predatory pricing. There are up to 8 marks for explaining up to four of these. The remaining 4 marks are for evaluation.

(d) To what extent is mail delivery contestable? (8 marks)

ⓔ This is a question about ease of entry and exit in an industry, and not about the level of competition. For 6 marks, explain why you think the market is or is not contestable, and for the evaluation (2 marks) consider the opposite case, or that the market is not as contestable or incontestable as initially explained.

(e) Evaluate whether further competition in public services would be in the best interests of consumers. (15 marks)

ⓔ For this question you will aim to consider why competition can work both in favour and against the interests of the consumer. You need to apply the theory to services beyond the current context. You could consider issues such as contracting out, competition within the Health Service, or other public–private partnerships such as PFI.

(a) Privatisation is a transfer of assets from the state to the private sector: 'part-privatisation is the only way to modernise Royal Mail and secure its long-term future' [a], which means that Royal Mail is going to have some parts owned by the private sector. This is supposed to bring efficiency in terms of 'providing management and technical expertise' [b].

[e] **5/5 marks awarded.** This type of answer requires the student only to refer to the extract to score full marks and does not require prior knowledge of the industry. [a] Clearly, this student shows evidence of having read the text and making reference to it. [b] The reasons for privatisation might be related to the problems involved, such as the requirement that the universal postal service continues.

(b) The firm is making more profit because costs have fallen. The firm is making heavy investment in technology, and it has become far more efficient in delivering mail. This is a fall in fixed costs. There is also a fall in variable costs, as post boxes are now only emptied once a day, and some households are having later deliveries as post workers have to work longer hours to complete more rounds with fewer workers.

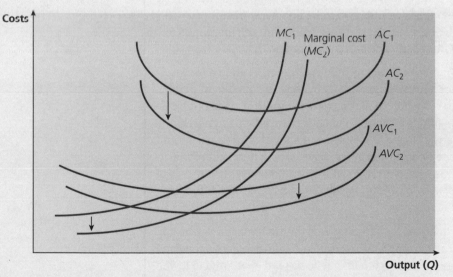

However, the profit rise might not last in the long run. Costs might start to rise in the future. Also there is a big fall in demand now that people use emails and social networking.

[e] **7/10 marks awarded.** The main problem here is that the diagram shows costs only and if profit is going to be shown (for which there is 1 mark), you will also need the revenue curves, AR and MR. The evaluation is correctly focused but needs to be fully explained.

(c) First, Royal Mail could introduce greater price discrimination, particularly between businesses and private individuals. Price discrimination increases profit by charging those individuals whose demand is less elastic more for the same service. Given that business customers' demand for mail services tends to be fairly inelastic, charging them more money could increase profits. Profits could also be increased by charging people on the basis of when they receive their mail. People who want their mail early in the morning tend to be business customers, whose demand for mail services is inelastic. Therefore, charging these customers more would increase profits.

ⓔ The student might have considered drawing a price discrimination diagram like that in Figure 23 on page 36. However, when drawing a diagram, consider whether it adds to the examiner's understanding. Most of the time the answer is 'Yes', but in this case, unless you can draw Figure 23 in 30 seconds, it would be an enormous waste of time and, therefore, potential marks.

In evaluation, we should note that there would be significant costs in implementing such a system. First, large registers of Royal Mail customers would need to be set up to determine what qualified as business mail and what was not business mail. Furthermore, the number of postal rounds would have to be doubled; there would have to be one early postal round and one later one. This would increase costs, thereby limiting the increases in profit resulting from an increase in price discrimination.

Second, Royal Mail could increase the amount it charges to send a letter. A great deal of mail has been made superfluous by the introduction of email. There is, therefore, little competition in the market for letter distribution because it is a rapidly declining industry. This gives Royal Mail significant price-making ability. Many of those who still send a lot of letters are people without computers. These people, therefore, have very inelastic demand for letter distribution. This means that Royal Mail could use its price-making ability to raise prices to consumers with inelastic demand, thereby increasing profit.

In evaluation, ⓐ it seems to be worth analysing who the customers are who send lots of letters. They are, by and large, businesses, government agencies and old people. Businesses and government agencies tend to attempt to lower their cost bases wherever possible, either to increase profits or because they are accountable to taxpayers. Therefore, if Royal Mail starts charging more, they will simply start using other letter distributors. Old people tend to live on fixed incomes and therefore minimise unnecessary spending. If the cost of sending a letter goes up, they will probably send fewer letters. Therefore, the price elasticity of demand for letter distribution appears to be much more elastic than first suggested, making raising prices for stamps a bad strategy for increasing Royal Mail's profitability.

ⓔ ⓐ In his or her evaluation, the student could also have considered the split in customer bases – how many of the consumers of Royal Mail are not business customers? Raising the price of stamps to the elderly may not be significant, even if demand from this group is relatively inelastic, as the group may represent a small proportion of the customer base.

> One non-price strategy that Royal Mail could introduce to improve its profitability would be to speed up the delivery of mail. Currently, Royal Mail loses a lot of money to courier firms, because many people like to have next-day delivery of their mail guaranteed, which Royal Mail cannot always do. By improving infrastructure, Royal Mail could speed up delivery and therefore win customers back from courier agencies, thereby increasing profits.
>
> In evaluation, this could increase Royal Mail's cost base. In order to improve the speed of mail delivery, Royal Mail would probably have to deploy more trains, vans and postmen. This would increase costs, thereby reducing the profitability of such an exercise.
>
> Another non-price strategy that Royal Mail could adopt to improve its profitability would be to reduce its cost base. Currently, Royal Mail has a high cost base. If Royal Mail were to reduce its workers' pay and fire excess labour, then it could reduce its labour costs and increase profits.

ⓔ 10/12 marks awarded. The reason this fails to score 12/12 is that 4 of the marks are allocated to evaluation in the mark scheme. Only a small percentage of the answer is devoted to this here.

This is an example of an excellent answer, which has been well structured and developed. The student has considered two pricing and two non-pricing strategies, all of which score well for their focus on Royal Mail.

> **(d)** A contestable market is one that is defined by low barriers to entry and exit and low sunk costs. ⓐ
>
> On the face of it, the market for mail distribution appears to be fairly incontestable. There are significant barriers to entry, in that Royal Mail is effectively subsidised by the government, ⓑ has massive brand power and benefits from significant economies of scale. Second, there are lots of barriers to exit, because workers cannot be fired without paying off their contracts.
>
> Sunk costs are those costs that cannot be retrieved upon exit from the market. There are very high sunk costs in the market for mail distribution because the industry is very labour intensive, and wages obviously cannot be recovered upon exit from the market. The machinery required for letter distribution is specific and is hard to sell on, given the fact that there are very few companies in the business.
>
> In evaluation, ⓒ we should point out that the barriers to entry are not as high as first supposed. First, the government's support for Royal Mail is dwindling, as shown by the passage. Second, Royal Mail's brand is often viewed with disdain by those who consider the company to be worn-out and inefficient. Finally, Royal Mail also suffers from significant diseconomies of scale. In these respects, the market may actually be fairly contestable.

ⓔ 7/8 marks awarded. **a** The definition at the beginning earns the first mark. This student has a good understanding of what is meant by contestability and applies it directly to Royal Mail. **b** The student does a good job of discussing the main issues that determine whether the mail delivery industry could be contestable, considering the types of sunk cost and attempting some evaluation. **c** However, more evaluation could have been provided, especially when considering the significance of the level of sunk costs and their relative importance, although there are two valid attempts.

> **(e)** On the one hand, competition should be in the interests of consumers. Competition should lead to lower prices for consumers, because firms have to compete to attract customers and will therefore lower price. Competition leads to a decrease in price-making ability and therefore to an increase in productive and allocative efficiency, as firms are forced to produce at the price set by the market. **a** However, this assumes that, with more competition, the market would move closer to the model of perfect competition. This is, of course, unrealistic. Given the complex, transnational nature of the letter distribution industry, it is unlikely that the market could support more than four or five firms. This would, in fact, make the market more like an oligopoly, giving the few firms that dominate the market the incentive to collude, to the detriment of the consumer.
>
> On the other hand, competition could have detrimental effects. **b** If a company has monopoly power, then it will be able to earn supernormal profits, which give it the means to increase research and development, and therefore to innovate. This can lead to new technologies emerging in mail distribution, which benefit the consumer. Second, if a company has monopoly power, it can benefit from economies of scale. Royal Mail benefits from significant financial economies of scale. Because it has systemic importance for the economy and is backed by the government, Royal Mail is a low credit risk and therefore benefits from relatively cheap loans. This lowers the prices that consumers pay.
>
> In evaluation, we should note that Royal Mail currently suffers from significant diseconomies of scale. It is so big and unwieldy that managers often have difficulty tracking mail going from one place to another. It has become so difficult logistically to control Royal Mail that it is now productively inefficient. If other firms were to take market share from Royal Mail as a result of competition, then it could become more efficient, benefiting consumers.

ⓔ 15/15 marks awarded. The student understands the need to consider both the benefits of increased competition and why competition might not work. **a** He or she describes some of the benefits one might expect with competition but recognises that, in the case of Royal Mail, this might not be beneficial, suggesting that Royal Mail may to an extent be a *natural* monopoly. **b** This leads on to a thoughtful discussion of why some industries are better off without competition, especially when competition leads to collusion among the dominant firms.

ⓔ Total: 44/50 marks. A good, clear grade A. The way to improve this answer is to develop each evaluation point to the full. Remember to make diagrams as helpful as possible.

Question 2 Tesco reports record £6.4bn loss

Extract 1 Supermarket company reports the worst results in its history and UK's biggest retail loss

Tesco has reported losses of £6.4bn, the worst result in its 96-year history and Britain's biggest-ever retail loss, after huge write-downs on the value of its property portfolio.

The annual result was worse than the City's most dire predictions that the group would fall £5bn into the red. Chief executive Dave Lewis said he had tried to make a break with Tesco's recent history by accounting for all likely events.

But Lewis warned that the food retail market remained 'challenging' and that despite signs of improving sales, Tesco's performance would be volatile for some time to come.

Lewis, who joined Tesco in September, said: 'We've got a long, long way to go and I don't think it will be smooth as we move through the changes we want to make. We have sought to draw a line under the past and to rebuild from here. Everything we know [about] we have dealt with.'

The former Unilever executive was drafted in to turn around the fortunes of Britain's biggest retailer following a series of profit warnings amid a ferocious price war with rivals. The sixth-biggest loss in UK corporate history is a far cry from results in recent years when Tesco's annual trading profits neared £4bn. Sales went into an alarming slide under Lewis's predecessor, Philip Clarke, who departed last year.

Clive Black, an analyst at Shore Capital, said: 'To say that Tesco had a nightmare year in 2015 would be an understatement, an out-turn that would simply have been unfathomable in days gone by.'

Black said there was little prospect of Tesco returning to the performance of its heyday but that Lewis and his team were doing the right things. 'The UK remains the priority and we see management basically saying that it is applying a plan that will take some time to come to fruition and investors will need to be patient,' Black said.

Tesco shares rose 1.3% to 238p in morning trading. They have gained 25% this year on hopes that Lewis can revive its fortunes, but the shares are still down by more than a third in the past two years.

The group has been caught up in a price war with rivals Asda, Sainsbury's and Morrisons as their market share is gnawed away by discounters Aldi and Lidl. Intense competition has exposed Tesco's over-expansion in the UK and declining standards at its stores.

Tesco's loss for the year to the end of February was the largest for a British retailer. The year before, the company reported an equivalent £2.3bn pre-tax profit. In UK stores open a year or more, sales excluding petrol fell 3.6% last year, but performance improved in the second half.

The biggest loss ever posted by a UK company was Royal Bank of Scotland's £24bn loss in 2008 after the bank was bailed out by the taxpayer. Tesco is now in sixth place in the losses league, behind Cable & Wireless's £6.5bn loss announced in 2003. It is the only retailer in the UK's top 10 biggest corporate losses, which also includes Vodafone and Lloyds Banking Group.

The main reason for Tesco's loss was a £4.7bn reduction in the value of its property holdings to reflect tough market conditions and declining profits. In total, Tesco took £7bn of one-off charges, more than wiping out a £1.4bn trading profit that was in line with reduced expectations.

Lewis said: 'It has been a very difficult year for Tesco. The results we have published today reflect a deterioration in the market and, more significantly, an erosion of our competitiveness over recent years. The market is still challenging and we are not expecting any let-up in the months ahead. When you add to this the fundamental changes we are making to our business and our offer, it is likely to lead to an increased level of volatility in short-term performance.'

Lewis said in January that he would close 43 stores and scrap plans to open 49 more. Some analysts have urged him to close hundreds more to recognise changed shopping habits as consumers buy online and skip the big weekly visit to the supermarket.

Lewis has also announced the closure of Tesco's head office in Cheshunt, Hertfordshire, and indicated that thousands of job losses were looming.

He has cut prices on hundreds of items and put more staff in stores in an attempt to lure back shoppers from Aldi and Lidl, whose prices were lower than Tesco's for many staple groceries and which did not rely on complicated promotional offers.

After years of growth in the UK, opening multiple shops close to each other, Tesco's strategy collapsed last year as it issued five profit warnings. Lewis, who is not a retailer by trade, was a surprise choice to replace Clarke, who was ousted as chief executive in July.

Soon after his arrival, Lewis unveiled a £263m accounting scandal caused by over-optimistic recording of payments made to Tesco by suppliers. Tesco is under investigation by the Serious Fraud Office and the supermarket regulator over the affair.

Lewis is considering selling businesses to reduce Tesco's debt after ratings agencies reduced the company to 'junk' status. He is in talks to sell all or part of the Dunnhumby analytics division that drives its Clubcard loyalty scheme. He said asking shareholders for cash was still an option.

Source: adapted from news sources

Figure A UK supermarket share in 2014

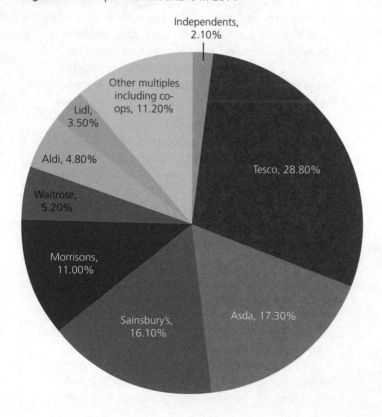

(a) With reference to the data, explain which market structure best describes the supermarket sector. (5 marks)

ⓔ When a question is asking about market structure, the answer is going to be perfect competition, monopolistic competition, oligopoly or monopoly, although sometimes more than one of these answers will be accepted. If there are any well-known or influential brand names such as Tesco, then it is unlikely to be either perfect or monopolistic competition. However, there are only 3 marks for identification and explanation of the market structure – the other 2 marks are *reserved* for application.

(b) To what extent can Tesco use its monopsony power to benefit the consumer? (8 marks)

ⓔ Note carefully that this question is about monopsony, not monopoly: it is about Tesco's buying power and its ability to drive down prices from its suppliers. If you find yourself talking about selling power, you will get no marks.

(c) Evaluate the likelihood of collusion in the supermarket industry. Use game theory to support your answer. (12 marks)

ⓔ Collusion refers to any kind of collaboration or co-operation between firms and it is always illegal, even though sometimes it is very difficult to detect. The aim of collusion is to increase the benefits to firms at the expense of consumers or other firms. Game theory is a multifunctional tool used by economists which analyses the reactions of some players in the market in response to others' actions. A payoff matrix is often used to simplify the possible outcomes and you will earn 2 marks if you use one effectively in the context provided. In order to evaluate these questions, it is crucial to stress the indeterminacy of outcomes, the problems of detection by the competition authorities and the unknown nature of the other players' reactions.

(d) Discuss the role the Competition and Markets Authority plays in protecting the public interest. (10 marks)

ⓔ The 1998 Competition Act makes any action by firms illegal if it is against the 'public interest'. This was reinforced in the 2002 Enterprise Act, which refers to substantial lessening of competition, stressing the nature of competition rather than the provable effects on consumers. The powers given to the regulatory authorities are significant: directors can be imprisoned and the firm fined up to 10% of its revenue over three years if found to be in breach of these acts. However, sometimes the illegalities are very difficult to prove, or the regulators might be 'taken in' by the firms, a situation known as 'regulatory capture' where the regulators choose not to report abuse. Sometimes the fines are not large enough to act as a deterrent, or the process of investigation might take so long that a ruling is out of date before it comes into force.

(e) Evaluate the impact of a demerger by Tesco and Dunnhumby on the firms, the workers and consumers. (15 marks)

ⓔ Demergers are important as part of section 3.1.2 business growth on the specification. You will hopefully read several exemplars similar to this as you prepare for your exam.

Student answer

(a) The market has a four-firm concentration ratio of 76.2%. The market is, therefore, best characterised as an oligopoly because it is dominated by a few large firms with significant price-making ability.

ⓔ 5/5 marks awarded. There is reference to and use of the data (2 marks), and clear reference to oligopoly with explanation (3 marks).

(b) Two points need to be analysed here. First, we need to examine how Tesco's monopsony power affects its cost base, and second we need to examine how changes in its cost base will translate into the price the consumer pays.

Monopsonies occur when a market has one large buyer and multiple sellers. This allows the buyer to drive down prices, as the sellers cannot sell to anyone, so they have to take the price offered by the buyer. This occurs with Tesco. Tesco has a degree of monopsony power; as the largest UK supermarket, Tesco can drive down the prices it pays for its products. Because farmers do not have many people to sell to, they will have to take the price Tesco offers them for their produce. This will cause the wholesale price of milk and other farm produce to fall, thereby lowering Tesco's cost base. This will allow Tesco to cut the prices that the consumer pays at the till.

However, if we continue our analysis, we will see that this is unlikely to happen. Tesco controls 31.4% of the UK food retail market. This affords Tesco significant price-making ability. In many areas of the UK, the only supermarket accessible to people is a Tesco store, giving it local monopoly power. Because Tesco has little competition, it may decide to use the purchasing economies of scale that emerge from its monopsony power to increase profits, rather than cut prices for consumers. It does not need to pass on price cuts, because it has monopoly power.

In evaluation, we should question the extent of Tesco's monopsony power. After all, 68.6% of the UK food retail market is controlled by retailers who are not affiliated with Tesco. Furthermore, producers could export their produce to other supermarkets within the EU. Therefore, they don't necessarily have to take the price that Tesco offers them, thus limiting Tesco's monopsony power.

ⓔ 7/8 marks awarded. An accurate definition of monopsony is given with reference to the data presented. There is a clear explanation of how the firm may actually use this power to drive down prices charged to them by farmers. Excellent linkages are made here to Tesco's monopoly position and therefore its price-setting power, as well as its position as a monopsony. This counts as evaluation, along with the reference to the extent to which Tesco has a monopsony. Top answers would have considered further the way in which Tesco could use its monopsony position to extract exclusivity deals and gain changes in delivery patterns and stock design.

(c) Collusion is best defined as tacit or explicit communication between competing companies that is to the detriment of the consumer.

On the one hand, collusion in the supermarket sector would appear to be very likely. Because the market has a four-firm concentration ratio of 76.2%, the market is characterised by oligopoly and therefore firms can collude with great ease – there are only four, so organising price fixing would not be hard. Furthermore, the incentives to collude are strong. If firms collude to fix prices, then there is no competition and the market has the characteristics of a monopoly – the firms that constitute the oligopoly can agree to fix prices where $MC = MR$, thereby maximising profits. Therefore, they can all benefit from higher prices. This is reflected on the game theory matrix in the upper-left quadrant, where the parties both co-operate, leading to both parties succeeding. The total payoff here is the largest the two firms could achieve working together. This is the highest possible payoff, reflecting the collectively rational position. Therefore, firms benefit the most from colluding.

If the other firm co-operates, it is better to defect and cut your prices, thereby undercutting the other firm, stealing its customers, increasing your profits and increasing your payoff on the matrix. If the other firm defects by cutting prices in spite of the agreement, it is better to defect and cut your prices too, so your customers will not be stolen by the other firm. Therefore, even if collusion is mutually beneficial, it is always in the interests of the firms in the agreement to lower their prices and take business from the other firms, so collusion is unlikely to function in the long term.

In evaluation, it is worth noting the other principal reason for which collusion is unlikely in the supermarket sector: the Office of Fair Trading (OFT). The OFT is a government agency that is mandated to prevent firms from engaging in uncompetitive practices that harm the consumer, such as price fixing and predatory pricing. If supermarkets all raise their prices in tandem without good justification, such as an increase in wholesale food prices, then the OFT can look into the price increases and fine them if it finds them to have engaged in price fixing. These fines can be very large and therefore act as a strong disincentive to collude.

ⓔ **12/12 marks awarded.** The student makes good use of the 2 × 2 matrix discussed on pages 31–32 of this book. The student clearly understands the implications of the 2 × 2 matrix, which suggests that there are clear incentives to be had from breaking any collusive agreement and trying to maximise your own individual benefits, especially before the authorities have been alerted to such behaviour.

(d) The Competition and Markets Authority is a government office that oversees mergers and acquisitions within the UK and prevents integration where it feels that it will be to the detriment of the consumer's interests.

The Competition and Markets Authority automatically oversees any merger that will give the resulting firm a share of the market that exceeds 25%. It may approve of mergers that give firms a large share of the market if it feels that this will lead to benefits to the consumer. Indeed, the CMA does seem to feel that mergers that create groups with large market share can be beneficial. The CMA allowed the acquisition of Colour Care Ltd by Kodak, on the grounds that the new firm would be more capable of fostering technological innovation, which would benefit the consumer.

The CMA does, however, remain wary of the dangers of certain mergers. When BSkyB tried to merge with Manchester United Football Club in 1998, the CMA prohibited the merger, on the grounds that it might lead to BSkyB charging high prices to watch pay-per-view footage of Manchester United games. This would have harmed the consumer; prices would have risen with no other benefits emerging, so the CMA prevented it.

In evaluation, we should note that the Competition and Markets Authority has been willing to play down the importance of competition in a difficult economic climate. The CMA approved the merger of Lloyds TSB with HBOS in 2008, despite the fact that the merger gave the new group significant price-making ability, because it felt that it was more important to safeguard the interests of Tesco investors.

ⓔ 6/10 marks awarded. The student makes reference to a number of examples from past Edexcel questions to support their answer and explain how the Competition and Markets Authority would seek to protect consumers. The student also refers to the Tesco application but only briefly. It must be stressed that this is a data-response exam and the use of data is critical for the application assessment objective. Lack of effective data use means that the answer is effectively capped on the KAA marks at 4/6 KAA. Top students could well have discussed the meaning of public interest and related it to the need for competition as determined by the Enterprise Act.

(e) The effect of a demerger for both Tesco and Dunnhumby is to make each firm smaller, which might mean the firms have less control in the market (reduction of market share) and reduces their monopoly power. This might make the businesses less profitable, but it might also make them more profitable if they become more efficient (they are likely to sell off their least profitable or loss-making parts).

Workers might lose out when in the demergers, especially those who have worked on the Dunnhumby side within the Tesco operation. Some workers might be forced to move location, if they are working in the headquarters of a part of a firm that changes in ownership, for example. They might even lose their job if the new owners find they have workers in similar roles already. However, because Dunnhumby is an online-based operation, many of the workers can work remotely or even from home, so there might not be a problem, and also they will be able to take on other work outside Tesco which might provide more scope for innovation and interest.

Consumers might not see any difference as the loyalty scheme will still be in place, but things might change in the long run or in a more subtle way, for example their loyalty card might change in name and in the way that it works, or benefits might reduce. But the long-term effect, if the merger is going to make Tesco more effective, might mean therefore lower prices and more choice for the consumer.

e **15/15 marks awarded.** There is excellent use of theory in the context of the data provided, and all points are evaluated.

e **Total: 45/50 marks.** A/A* border.

Question 3 Trains in Britain cost 50% more than in rest of Europe

Extract 1 Cost of rail fares in Britain

This study reveals that rail fares in Britain are on average 50% higher than the rest of Europe, putting pressure on rail operators and the government to cut ticket prices. Annual season tickets for middle-distance commuters are almost double the price of the next most expensive country, France, and more than four times that of the cheapest country, Italy.

Passenger Focus, focusing on consumer interests, carried out the inquiry in 2008. Ruth Kelly MP had noticed that customer satisfaction levels had not risen in line with improvements in train performance. Anthony Smith, chief executive of Passenger Focus, says the study confirms that British fares are 'astonishingly expensive, especially for tickets that you buy on the day and especially for commuters in London and the south-east'.

However, it is not all bad news for British travellers. Passengers willing to make advance purchases can buy some of the cheapest tickets available in Europe and British trains run more frequently, with passenger services starting earlier and finishing later than their continental rivals. The findings bring new calls for the government to revise plans to cut rail subsidies. The government aims to get passengers to pay 75% of the cost of operating and improving the network – a rise from £5 billion per year now to £9 billion by 2014.

'The government should review its intention to shift the cost of funding the railway from taxpayers to passengers, said Mr Smith. 'Passengers cannot be expected to continue paying above-inflation fare increases year on year during the recession.'

Source: Passenger Focus inquiry commissioned by Ruth Kelly MP, adapted from www.passengerfocus.org.uk/

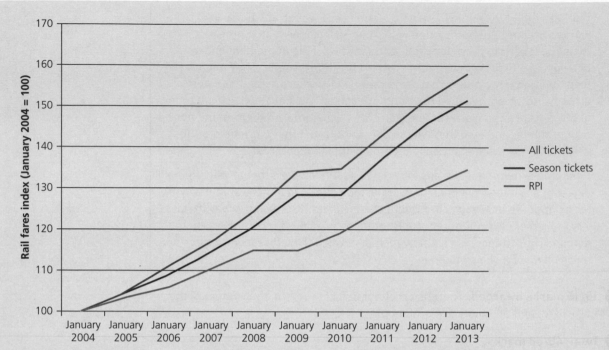

Figure 1 The cost of train fares and season tickets has risen above inflation for at least a decade

Source: The Office of Rail and Road

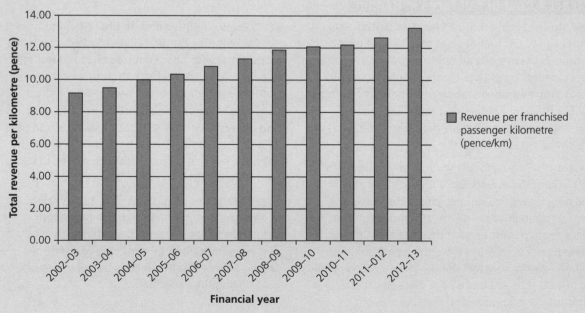

Figure 2 The amount of money made by rail companies on each kilometre travelled has increased every year since 2002

Source: The Office of Rail and Road

(a) What is meant by a 'natural monopoly'? (5 marks)

e Natural monopoly is an important aspect of the topic 'monopoly'. It occurs where economies of scale make it efficient when there is just one firm operating and increasing the number of firms makes average costs increase.

(b) Discuss whether wider use of regulation may benefit railway passengers. (12 marks)

e Regulation refers to the intervention by governments to control the actions of firms when there is a perception or observation that firms are working in a way that is detrimental to the consumer and efficiency in general. In this case, there is no competition between railway track providers to keep costs down, so the government uses regulation as a surrogate for competition and to ensure that prices are kept down and that service is of a reasonable quality. Price caps are an important control, e.g. *RPI – X*, but there are other forms of regulation that you need to know. (*RPI* is a measure of inflation that you will have come across in Theme 2.)

(c) Evaluate the impact of a reduction in the state-provided subsidy for the railway companies. (8 marks)

e The functions of subsidies are to keep firms in business if they provide a valuable output or a major form of employment and to keep prices down for consumers. The main problem with subsidies is that they allow firms to become inefficient and they inhibit consumer choice by lowering the price of goods and services that consumers would not otherwise buy. So the effect of removing subsidies is to put this argument in reverse, and in this case it needs to be applied to railways, for example by saying that without the subsidy the railways might not run on unprofitable routes.

(d) Assess the potential benefits of price capping as a method of controlling monopolies. (10 marks)

e Evaluating benefits can involve considering the problems or weaknesses of price caps, and also alternatives to price caps such as increasing the contestability of the market by deregulation.

(e) Assess why rail prices in the UK might be significantly higher than those in the rest of the EU. (15 marks)

e For a 15-mark question, the safest policy is to choose three points and to evaluate them all. In this case, it may be difficult to find enough points, especially if you feel that this is an area in which you do not have any particular knowledge. Use concepts such as elasticities and subsidies, but remember that you need to develop them as much as you can.

Student answer

(a) A natural monopoly is a monopoly that occurs naturally in an economy because the market cannot support more than one firm. The railways are an example of a natural monopoly because there is only one railway company – Network Rail – which supplies the tracks. There are really high costs to setting up a rival firm and no one would try to establish another rail line because it will cost lots and take a long time before any expenditure is recovered.

ⓔ **2/5 marks awarded.** This student has some understanding of what is meant by a natural monopoly but lacks the technical expertise that one would expect to see from an A-grade student, such as reference to high barriers to entry and high sunk costs. This answer would benefit from a diagram (see Figure 24), which could be used to explain and support the answer.

(b) Prices can be regulated using the *RPI – X* formula in order to ensure that prices may increase in nominal terms, but they will tend to fall in real terms. The regulator will set prices in such a way as to ensure that the train operator will be able to make a profit, but will have to make efficiency savings and improvements in quality if they are to increase their profits. This will happen because the train operator can keep any profits they make after they have cut costs.

The benefits of this system are that it allows the rail operator to keep any profits that it makes, but ensures that there is an incentive to improve the quality of service and to get more passengers on board the trains. However, it is quite possible that a cut in costs will equate to a cut in customer service, as the drive to make efficiency gains and increase profits to satisfy the demands of shareholders outweighs the desire to maintain quality of service, particularly as demand for trains is often seen to be relatively price inelastic.

ⓔ **7/12 marks awarded.** The main weakness is that the student does not refer to other types of regulation such as performance targeting or requirements to invest in track – price controls in isolation are just one strand of regulation.

The student discusses quality of service but could also have mentioned regulatory capture as one possible downside of regulation; they could have tried to compare the UK method of regulation with other types of regulation (these are now included in the specification) or mentioned the need for rail operators to spend on capital and therefore referred to the possibility of using *RPI + K*.

(c) The subsidy received from the state helps to ensure that prices remain low and therefore encourage consumers to use the railways. A reduction in the state subsidy is, therefore, likely to put pressure on the train operators either to cut costs or raise prices. As they have probably been forced to cut costs by the regulator over the years, it is clear that the only feasible alternative is to raise prices. This will put pressure on already hard-pressed consumers. They are likely to consider alternatives to the train, although road transport is also becoming more expensive and therefore less attractive. The state has been keen to reduce the size of the subsidy for some time, encouraging the private sector to take greater responsibility for the cost of running the railways, but this will no doubt put some routes that the private sector runs under even greater pressure. It is much harder for the state to force firms to run loss-making routes and cross-subsidise these with the profits from other routes if the state makes no contribution. Undoubtedly at some point, consumers will feel resentful over the fact that service has declined and they have to pay more so that they can provide a service that they are unlikely ever to need.

ⓔ 5/8 marks awarded. This is a good answer, which addresses the main issues surrounding a reduction in the subsidy and the possible outcomes in the form of resentment, loss of certain routes, poorer customer service and higher prices. The student could also have considered whether the subsidy was actually needed any more and whether the firms were now in a position to stand on their own feet.

Furthermore, the subsidy could have acted as a disincentive to improve efficiency and it is only with this reduction that the firms can improve. Although prices have been rising and are the highest in Europe, this has not yet had an effect on demand and it may be possible to raise prices further without consumer demand declining significantly.

(d) Price capping is used to regulate many firms in the UK. The price cap is an upper limit for the price increase that the firms can add to their prices, using the level of inflation measured by the retail price index, and then takes account of possible efficiency gains (given the value X) or investment that the firm needs to make (K).

One advantage of price capping is that it allows a firm to keep profits it makes through bringing about greater efficiency gains than the regulator has required. In addition, because the X or K factors are usually in place for a capping period of five or more years, firms are able to plan ahead and know that they will be able to keep the benefits from making further efficiency gains.

However, if the regulator underestimates the value of X, then the railway firms can make enormous profits as indicated in the passage, but they argue that these are used to invest in areas outside the regulator's remit and therefore generate even greater profits in the future. Sometimes the regulator and the firm it is regulating have an interdependent relationship, resulting in the regulator being less strict on the firms under its control. This close relationship is referred to as regulatory capture.

ⓔ 6/10 marks awarded. This answer is technically accurate, but it is not applied to the context (there are 1/3 application marks awarded) and the evaluation is not extended to show why price capping is not the best method. It would be better to bring in other forms of regulation (2/4 for evaluation).

(e) Rail prices in Britain are the highest in Europe. The article states that prices in the UK are almost double those of France, the next most expensive supplier, and almost four times the price of the Italian railways. This may be the case for a number of reasons.

It may be the case that the subsidy in the UK is significantly less than that of the other members of the European Union and therefore rail passengers must pay a larger proportion of the cost of operating the railways.

On the other hand it may be the case that the railways in Britain have invested larger amounts to ensure a better quality of train and service. This may be the reason why British trains run more frequently and are more punctual.

Furthermore, consumers may be willing to pay more for the railways because there are few reliable and price-competitive substitutes. The car may be a more expensive alternative and the establishment of the congestion charge and increased traffic means that the demand for the railways is relatively price inelastic.

ⓔ 10/15 marks awarded. The student has managed to identify three reasons why the prices may be higher in Britain compared with the rest of Europe, but there is no evaluation. It earns 2 + 2 + 2, although the last point on inelasticity could be developed fully to secure a third or fourth mark. Evaluation is needed to show which factors are most important and make judgements about the points made. It may have included some reference to profiteering or a benign regulator allowing the train operators to raise prices. It may also be the case that the train-operating companies are colluding to fix prices and therefore maximise their own profits. Government subsidies clearly play a role, but are these the most significant factor? Perhaps British rail operators run more cost-ineffective services (the article states that they are more frequent) than their European rivals and so need to recoup the cost through higher prices.

Total: 30/50 marks. Grade C. The lack of evaluation here damages the student's mark. Evaluation is crucial in ensuring that a student accesses the full range of marks and achieves a top grade.

Question 4 Poundland and 99p Stores' proposed buyout

Extract 1 Statement from Poundland

Poundland Group plc, Europe's leading single-price general merchandise retailer, sells branded and own-label products at the single price point of £1. It also comprises the 'Dealz' brand in Ireland, with products sold at €1.49. In September 2015 Poundland announced that it had signed a conditional sale and purchase agreement for Poundland to acquire 99p Stores for an enterprise value of £55 million, comprising a cash consideration of £47.5 million and the issue of new Poundland shares with a value of £7.5m at current share prices on the FTSE (280p), on 6 February 2015.

Poundland believes that the combination of the two businesses will provide better choice, value and service for 99p Stores' customers. Poundland currently operates a network of 580 stores in the UK and Ireland, and is targeting another 500 new stores in its long-term plan, both through horizontal integration and through setting up stores in new venues. Poundland Group plc shares have risen 22% since the deal was announced.

The proposed transaction includes 99p Stores' network of 251 stores (trading as '99p Stores' and 'Family Bargains'), which serve more than 2 million customers a week, as well as its warehouse and distribution centre. In the year to 1 February 2014, 99p Stores had sales of £370.4 million, underlying earnings of £54 million, gross assets of £91.2 million and net assets of £11.2 million and a profit margin of 36.9%.

When the two businesses are fully integrated, the proposed transaction is expected to enhance earnings per share for Poundland's shareholders, and long-term profitability prospects will improve.

The costs associated with the integration and restructuring of 99p Stores will be funded by a share issue to be undertaken at or immediately prior to the closing of the transaction and an increase in Poundland's revolving credit facilities, reflecting its focus on preserving a conservative financial profile to support the capital investment plans in its business. The Acquisition is conditional on the approval of the Competition and Markets Authority ('CMA'). Given the size and market share of the two companies, the CMA will review the proposed transaction and Poundland and 99p Stores have already held discussions with the CMA regarding the proposed takeover.

Source: adapted from www.poundland.co.uk/corporate-information/

Extract 2 Poundland and 99p Stores merger faces in-depth investigation unless suitable undertakings offered

The anticipated acquisition by Poundland plc of 99p Stores Limited will be referred for an in-depth investigation by the CMA – unless acceptable undertakings are offered. Poundland and 99p Stores are two large national discount retail chains with a combined network of around 800 stores located throughout the UK. They both supply general merchandise at a single price point, ranging from stationery, homeware, gardening and seasonal merchandise to groceries and other fast-moving consumer goods – meeting the needs of a wide range of customers who seek convenience and value at low and consistent prices. Poundland and 99p compete closely and can be distinguished from other value general merchandisers since they sell nearly all products at a single price point.

Following an initial investigation, the Competition and Markets Authority (CMA) has found that the transaction gives rise to a realistic prospect of a substantial lessening of competition in 80 local areas where the companies currently overlap – and in a further 12 areas where they will be competitors in the near future.

The CMA found that the parties are each other's closest competitors and that after the transaction they will only face close competition from one other single price retailer with national scale, Poundworld, and from other discounted retailers such as B&M, Home Bargains, Wilko and Poundstretcher.

In the problematic areas, the parties will only be constrained by three or less of their competitors and it is so far unclear whether they would provide the same level of competition that currently exists between Poundland and 99p.

The CMA found that the loss of competition between the companies may lead to a worsening of their offer locally, through a reduction in quality, fewer promotions or closure of their stores. The transaction will therefore be referred for an in-depth phase 2 investigation by an independent group of CMA panel members unless the parties offer acceptable undertakings to address the CMA's competition concerns in a clear-cut manner.

Sheldon Mills, CMA Senior Director of Mergers and decision maker in this case, said: 'As consumers become ever-more price conscious, they value the low prices offered by these retailers and their shopping around for bargains is aided by the simplicity of their pricing. After the merger, Poundland will no longer face competition from its closest rival, and following our initial investigation, it is unclear whether the constraint posed by remaining retailers is sufficiently strong to mitigate our concerns over how the transaction might affect choice, value and service for shoppers. Without competition from 99p Stores, there is the possibility that Poundland may have the incentive and ability to deteriorate its offer in these areas to the disadvantage of customers that have come to rely on their offer. Given the potential impact on customers, we will now open a detailed investigation into this merger unless the parties offer suitable undertakings.'

(a) Explain which market structure national discount retail chains in the UK seem to operate in.   (5 marks)

e Market structures include perfect competition, monopolistic competition, oligopoly and monopoly. Very few answers that have famous firms such as this will be either perfect competition or monopolistic competition, so the choice is very narrow.

(b) Assess ways in which the Poundland and 99p Stores merger represents a principal–agent problem. (10 marks)

ⓔ A new kind of question based on a new element of the specification, and one in which candidates will struggle to relate textbook learning to the context.

(c) Apart from integration, discuss one non-pricing strategy that national discount retail chains might use to prevent further losses. Use game theory to support your answer. (12 marks)

ⓔ Game theory is used to model the behaviour of interdependent agents. It can take many forms. You might want to use a payoff matrix or Sweezy's kinked demand curve. There are several other valid approaches, too.

(d) Discuss the potential benefits of horizontal integration of firms in a market where profit margins are falling. (8 marks)

ⓔ This is a standard question on integration (most people will refer to economies of scale and increased market share) but with a twist – it must be related to falling profit margins.

(e) National discount retail chains such as Poundland and 99p Stores were investigated by the Competition and Markets Authority (CMA) in 2015 before the merger was allowed to take place. Discuss possible issues the CMA might face when attempting to regulate this industry. (15 marks)

ⓔ Remember that for this question you must make at least three if not four good solid points. It is a contextual question and you should show your understanding that market conditions have noticeably changed since the start of the credit crunch in 2007 when, in the UK, many firms went out of business. The context is important for this question.

> **Student answer**
>
> **(a)** The market structure of the national discount retail chains is an oligopoly. An oligopoly is a market where there are many firms, with three to eight firms dominating the market. ⓐ There are high barriers to entry and exit, and firms supply similar products. Firms like Poundland, 99p Stores and Costcutters dominate the industry. ⓑ

ⓔ **2/5 marks awarded.** ⓐ The student earns 1 mark for correctly identifying oligopoly, but the explanation is not entirely convincing. There are unlikely to be *many* firms, if there are just three to eight firms! A better approach would be to say 'a few firms dominate the market'. Another approach is to use the rule of thumb that 'five or fewer firms control at least 50% of the market'.

ⓑ The application marks are 1 out of 2 marks. The application simply lists the national discount retail chains, it does not actually identify any of the barriers to entry or exit, such as strong brand loyalty in the national discount retail chains.

(b) In cases where there are a large number of shareholders, the day-to-day management of the business is delegated to a board of directors and from them to their managers, and in the case of the Poundland shareholders, there is little they can do to affect the amount that they receive as a result of their risk taking and how much profit is reinvested into the firm after the merger takes place. In such cases there can be problems associated with divorce of ownership, known as the principal–agent problem. The principal is the shareholder of Poundland, while the person in charge of the day-to-day running of the business is referred to as the agent (the directors of Poundland). In such cases the agent can make decisions on behalf of the business that do not necessarily match the direction in which the owners would like to take the business. This can be a problem if the principal is not fully aware of the actions of the agent, as is often the case with large corporations, or they lack sufficient information, as a result of asymmetric information. In such instances the directors can behave in a way that conflicts with the objectives of the owners.

When the two businesses are fully integrated, the proposed transaction is expected to enhance earnings per share for Poundland's shareholders, meaning that the principal is likely to gain some increased dividend. However, there are going to be many more shareholders as a result of the 'equity placing', in order to raise the cash consideration of £47.5 million and the cash costs associated with the integration and restructuring of 99p Stores. The firm is preserving a 'conservative financial profile to support the capital investment plans in its business'. This may result in the agent being rewarded if the investment is successful, and the agent's pay might be enhanced by bonuses if successful. However, there could be a problem if there are hidden costs or if for other reasons the share price or dividend falls, in which case the decision to merge would not have been taken by the principal, if the full risks were known.

10/10 marks awarded. This is a difficult area to discuss, and the data are used carefully to explain the problem and also to discuss the idea that it might not be a problem – thus also earning the 4 evaluation marks.

(c) A non-pricing strategy that national discount retail chains could have used to prevent further losses would be to collude with one or more firms in order to fix prices. If firms that dominate a market agree to both increase the price of their product, both firms will experience an increase in revenue, which might cause one firm such as Poundland to start making a profit and so would therefore prevent further losses. Neither firm would lose much market share because if both firms increase their prices then customers will have nowhere else to go to and so revenue will just rise.

However, if both firms have increased their prices, then each firm will have a financial incentive to lower their own prices in order to capture market share from the other firm and increase the amount of revenue that the firm will receive. This behaviour is called game theory and can be represented with a matrix.

		Firm Y	
		Collude	Not collude
Firm X	**Collude**	Firm X gets £10 million Firm Y gets £10 million £20 million combined	Firm X gets £14 million Firm Y gets £3 million £17 million combined
	Not collude	Firm X gets £14 million Firm Y gets £3 million £17 million combined	Firm X gets £5 million Firm Y gets £5 million £10 million combined

As we can see, if both firms colluded, the combined revenue would be maximised at £20 million, for example. However, firms will tend towards the maximax in order to maximise their own welfare and so will break their collusion by lowering prices so that one firm can achieve revenues of £14 million, leaving the other firm with only £3 million. The other firm will then respond to this by also lowering its prices and so both firms will end up at the maximin or the Nash equilibrium, where the combined revenue is minimised at £10 million and both firms will be worse off, but before any further agreements are reached this is the position they will logically reach.

ⓔ 5/12 marks awarded. Collusion is a good choice of non-price competition strategy. However, there is a logical problem in using the payoff matrix in this way. If X colludes with Y – that is, if it collaborates – then surely Y also colludes with X. So the labels for the matrix are ill-thought through. It would perhaps be best to put in 'collude' and 'cheat' so that for the second option firm Y might act as a whistle-blower, let firm X get fined heavily, and then gain from going its own way in the short run.

The second problem is that, although the word 'however' is used, there is not any evidence of evaluation. Evaluation could be in the form of saying *why* your conclusions might not hold, or whether other things are not equal.

1 out of 2 marks for payoff matrix, 2 for application to extract (which is done effectively), 2 marks for correct analysis of game theory and 0 for evaluation.

(d) Horizontal integration is where a firm merges with another that is at the same stage of production within the same industry.

If a firm merges with another firm at the same stage of production, that firm could benefit from managerial economies of scale where, as the firm expands, it is in a better position to employ specialist managers aiming to increase productivity, reducing long-run average costs and so therefore increasing the profit margin gained by the firm.

However, the firm may actually experience diseconomies of scale if this does not work properly. Bringing in new management may cause a conflict in ideologies and so managers may be concentrating too much on debating rather than actually increasing the productivity of the firm and so long-run average costs may actually increase, further reducing the profit margin.

Another benefit that the integration may bring is an increase in sales due to an increase in brand recognition. Brand recognition would increase because the firm would take on the customer base of the other firm and so more people would be exposed to the brand name of the firm. This would increase people's trust in the brand name and so sales would increase, causing revenue to also increase.

However, there are many costs associated with integration. When two firms merge, there has to be some sort of restructuring and this would mean that redundancies would have to be made and so there would be redundancy costs that the firm has to pay. If a firm took over another firm within the national discount retail chains industry, that firm would have to pay the cost of rebranding all the other firm's branches with its own brand and so with all these initial costs, it may only be in the long run that firms actually experience an increase in profits and in the short run may actually have to incur a loss.

ⓔ 8/8 marks awarded. This answer clearly earns full marks. A good balance between knowledge, application and analysis (KAA) and evaluation.

(e) The Competition and Markets Authority regulates the markets and acts in the interest of the consumer by promoting competition and so maximising consumer welfare. They can issue fines to firms that take part in anti-competitive behaviour. **ⓐ**

The merger between national discount retail chains would have caused Poundland's market share to be above the legal definition of a monopoly, which is a market share of above 25%. This would therefore cause a reduction in competition within the national discount retail chains industry and so the Competition and Markets Authority had to intervene in order to protect the welfare of the consumers.

In late 2008 however, the global economic crisis hit and the UK high street was in turmoil, with many firms going out of business and the UK high street having up to 1 in 3 empty retail outlets. The merging of firms might be for the benefit of the consumer and it is very hard for the CMA to know if the firms will gain from economies of scale or will use their monopoly power to exploit the consumer. The acquisition would also be in the best interest of the nation if prices are lower, with an increase in availability of stores, but it is difficult for the CMA to know the future state of the economy and what the consumer will have left in their pockets to spend. **ⓑ**

However, with the benefit of hindsight, we know that this merger has caused many problems within the national discount retail chains because Poundland has a huge market share and makes almost a billion pounds in profits each year. It has been able to set prices high and capture consumer welfare. In reaction to this, the Competition and Markets Authority has looked at whether the takeover will in fact increase their monopsony power because they will be able to buy their supplies at much lower prices.

> Another issue is that consumer welfare may actually increase because a bigger firm would be able to survive the changing economic climate and so would be able to provide service to consumers who need it, and can keep prices down when incomes are so low.

e **10/15 marks awarded.** a The answer defines the role of the Competition and Markets Authority accurately, for 1 mark. b The application is secure and the theory of the workings of the competition authorities is applied effectively to the discount retail industry. The main problem is that this answer runs out of time, and after the first main point, the answer tumbles out a few more options. The best advice to this student is to make a plan of three or four factors and spread the time evenly for them. The marks dwindle, as does the length of the paragraphs, and only 1 mark can be awarded for the last two paragraphs respectively. 4 + 1 + 1 for KAA and 4 for evaluation = 10 marks.

Total: 35/50 marks. A grade (but near B border).

■ Paper 1 and Paper 3

Open-extended questions

The 25-mark essay questions on all A-level papers (1 to 3) are a choice from two and will be 'stretch and challenge' questions. On Paper 1 they will be synoptic based on Themes 1 and 3, and on Paper 3 they will allow you to draw from microeconomics and macroeconomics, Themes 1 to 4. You might find from past papers that you are directed to cover both micro and macro for Paper 3, but this is not guaranteed, and it might be that you will be able to specialise in your answers.

It is important as you progress through your second year of study of Economics A that you start to practise synoptic questions. For this reason we introduce a Paper 3 here, but it should be noted that not all of this paper is based on microeconomics and therefore the student answer is just focused on this part for the purposes of this guide.

Question 1 Paper 1 Section C Labour markets and government intervention in industry

e NB Paper 1 Section C starts with question 7 and you choose between questions 7 and 8. In Paper 3 the essay questions are 1 and 2 (d) and (e), but the essay section is numbered question 1 here for ease of understanding.

Either

(1) Evaluate the reasons why the government might set a maximum wage. (25 marks)

Or

(2) Evaluate the likely labour market effects of labour market immobility. Use the concepts of the elasticity of demand and supply of labour in your answer. (25 marks)

Student answer

(1) A maximum wage could prevent the highest income people from increasing their salaries at the expense of other workers. For example, in 2015 some NHS locum doctors were earning £400000 while other parts of the NHS were unable to operate owing to lack of funds to keep wards clean and nurses to cover the duties. The government has announced measures to clamp down on 'rip-off' staffing agencies used by the NHS to plug gaps in nursing and doctor rotas. It will set a maximum hourly rate for temps and cap the amount trusts that are struggling financially can spend. The agencies say they are being blamed for the NHS's own mismanagement of workforce planning but one solution would be to impose a maximum pay for temp workers. NHS foundation trusts in England spent nearly £2bn last year on agency staff.

On one occasion, an agency nurse cost the NHS £2200 for a 12-hour shift, and a doctor £3700 for a 30-hour shift. In some instances, more than half of the money went to the agency itself. And hospitals are increasingly hiring expensive management consultants, which cost the NHS nearly £600m last year.

In the UK there are measures which will be phased in over the next few months and include a cap of £50000 applied to all management-consultancy contracts. Currently, many NHS trusts manage their agency spend through framework agreements that cap prices. Rates are negotiated by central government, and recruitment agencies should adhere to them.

But under the new measures, agencies charging the market rate will be barred from use, but the rate is formed by market forces, and a pay cap might only mean there are shortages of these workers.

At the same time, the pay of some NHS senior managers will also be cut. Currently, more than a fifth of all directors in the NHS earn more than £142500 – the amount the Prime Minister is paid. The NHS is a public service and there is an opportunity cost in the NHS for paying such high wages to specialist and agency staff, and it needs to show restraint on handing out generous pay packages. A pay cap means more money could be spent elsewhere. Private companies are charging up to £3,500 a shift for a doctor. The NHS is bigger than all of these agencies, so they can use their monopsony power (bargaining power with agencies) to drive down rates of agency specialist staff.

However, the rising costs are partly due to hospitals putting more nurses on wards, following the public inquiry into the Stafford Hospital scandal. Other arguments are the government mismanagement of the NHS, and the use of PFI for contracts which are cheap in the short term but in the long term have to be paid for at high rates.

ⓔ A rather narrow answer in that it is only focused on the NHS, but an effective attempt to apply data and explain the context. A question such as this does not require a diagram, but it would be credited and would be a very valuable way to earn both application and analysis marks.

This answer is very evaluative in the sense that there are many judgements, but there should be several evaluative approaches, each point including some application and analysis of its own.

KAA Level 3, 10/16. Evaluation Level 1, 3/9. Total 13/25 = Grade C.

---

(2) The inability to move between jobs is called labour immobility, and there are two main kinds, geographical and occupational.

One of the impacts of immobility is structural unemployment. This occurs when there is a mismatch of skills in the labour market. It can be caused by occupational immobilities, which refer to the difficulties in learning new skills applicable to a new industry and technological change, e.g. an unemployed tobacco farmer may struggle to find work as a biochemist at Nestlé. It can also be from geographical immobilities, which is about the difficulty in moving regions to get a job. For example, there may be jobs in London, but it may be difficult to find affordable housing for the worker's children. In addition, it could be caused by technological change, where if there is the development of labour-saving technology in some industries, there would be a fall in demand for labour. A structural change in the economy could cause it as well. The decline of the London Docklands due to the lack of competitiveness meant that many dockers were unemployed. They found it very difficult to find jobs in new industries such as computer technology.

Elasticity of demand for labour refers to the responsiveness of demand to changes in the wage rate. If demand is said to be price inelastic (referring to the price of labour, or wages), then if wages were to increase the impact on demand would be limited. This is typical in industries where workers are skilled and cannot be easily replaced with either cheaper workers or capital equipment. On the other hand, when the demand for labour is wage elastic, then an increase in wages is likely to result in a large decrease in the demand for labour, often replacing workers with capital equipment.

The wage elasticity of demand for labour will depend on cost of the worker required relative to the overall cost of running the business, but also the time it takes to implement other processes and of course how long the period is under consideration. In the short term it is usually hard to replace labour, so demand tends to be wage inelastic, but in the long run it can be replaced, for example with machines, so the demand for labour tends to be wage elastic. Elasticity of supply of labour refers to the responsive of workers or potential workers to changes in the wage rate. If supply is said to be price inelastic (again referring to wages), then if wages were to increase the impact on supply would be limited. This is typical in industries where workers take time to acquire skills or training and cannot easily enter the market. So if there are many rigidities in the labour market the firm is likely to have to pay much higher wages.

If a particular job requires a number of years' training and specific skills, then the price or wage elasticity of supply is relatively inelastic, so even if demand increases for that job it will take time for the labour market to respond. An example is teachers who require not just a degree but certain skills in expressing their ideas clearly and a way of engaging with children, many of which need time to develop if indeed they can be taught at all! If people are just 'born teachers' then supply is relatively inelastic so wages increase. However, in the long run additional training will mean that teachers become relatively more in number and so as wages increase there is a steady stream of people able to work at a high level of specialism in the teaching profession, making supply relatively wage elastic in the long run. Clearly, in such instances, living in a global market will mean that the economy can recruit from abroad, using migration to increase the supply of workers, helping to plug the skills shortage and keep wages from increasing, as well as satisfying the increased demand.

So in evaluation a low *PED* and *PES* in the labour markets is a main cause of the problems of structural unemployment, and the inequality in wages. However, governments can use long-term training schemes, buy to let and other forms of subsidy to encourage workers into a profession over time (increase the *PES*) and can encourage firms to retrain and relocate workers (increase their *PED*) rather than replace the workers with machines.

e 22/25 marks awarded. Overall, this student secures 22/25 marks despite the time pressures because there are two evaluation points, explained in the context and again at the end. The application to the market for teachers makes it an interesting read for the examiner! The only real weakness is the lack of analysis and broader application, which could be achieved with a diagram.

Question 2 Paper 3 Sections A and B synoptic questions

The following is a section of a sample Paper 3, focusing on the Theme 3 elements of the paper. You could use this whole paper for exam practice for Paper 3, but bear in mind that more data would be provided for the macroeconomic elements.

Save this question until the final revision period before your Paper 3 exam because it tests a whole range of skills and knowledge. You would be advised to produce an answer under timed conditions and get someone else to read it back to you. You might be surprised at how different your answers sound when read aloud. It is a useful technique, not least because examiners tend to do this with answers at standardisation meetings when the mark is not immediately agreed. The better the quality of your communication, the more likely the examiners will warm to the logic you employ. Exams are a combat of the pen: engage your weapons with sure strokes, a clear strategy and a fully thought-out response to counter-argument.

Question 2 Venezuela's economy

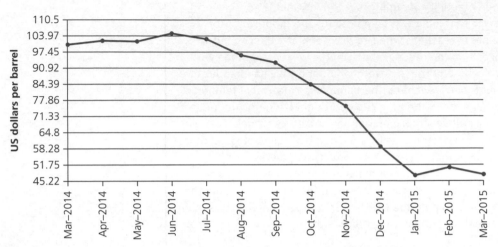

Figure 1 World oil prices, using the Brent crude measure, 2013–14
Source: www.tinyurl.com/on39krf

Extract 1 Falling world oil prices

Oil prices are plunging as the OPEC cartel has lost, or given up, its control of the market. In other words, it is not making an effort to relieve the oil supply glut that has been keeping prices low.

At the moment, falling energy prices are effectively a tax break for the US consumer. Longer term, the danger might be a huge price swing in the other direction, especially if today's low prices force many unprofitable producers to shut down in the next year or so. Losing too much investment could create a price shock in future years as necessary supply growth cannot return quickly once curtailed. Moreover, as prices fall, the risk of power failure rises, particularly in financially stressed nations that cannot maintain subsidies.

President Nicolás Maduro has insisted the current oil price falls will not harm Venezuela's economy or its social spending plans. The oil price fall was putting pressure on consumer incomes, export revenues and the value of the currency. Venezuela is suffering from inflation of 63%, fuelled by government currency controls, which have created a booming unofficial or 'black' currency market and led to severe shortages in the shops of essential consumer goods such as milk and toilet paper. So although petrol is cheap, Venezuela is suffering from inflation.

Source: adapted from www.tinyurl.com/qjq5twg and www.tinyurl.com/nh44avx

(a) With reference to Figure 1, Extract 1 and your own knowledge, explain the main influences on investment.

(5 marks)

ⓔ This is essentially a macro question, which is covered in the Theme 2 Student Guide.

(b) Using a short-run average cost and revenue diagram, examine the likely impact of falling oil prices on the profits of firms that use a large quantity of energy in their production processes.

(8 marks)

(e) This question follows a similar style to those in the old 6EC03 paper. You would be rewarded for using a shift in revenues if you argue that all firms are cutting their prices and demand is relatively inelastic, but the standard response the examiner expects is that you argue that the *AVC* and *MC* shift downwards. *MC* has to shift as well as *AVC* because oil is a variable production cost. Remember also to focus your answer on profit, not just the costs of the firm.

Remember that there are 2 marks for evaluation. You might consider the degree of the oil price change (it fell by more than 50%) or the fact that it was only short term (oil prices have risen since then), among the many possible approaches.

(c) With reference to Figure 1 and Extract 1, discuss the reasons for the changes in the exchange rate of the Venezuelan bolivar against the US dollar.   (12 marks)

(e) This is essentially a macro question, with concepts covered in the Theme 4 Student Guide.

Either

(d) With reference to the information provided and your own knowledge, evaluate the likely microeconomic and macroeconomic impact of the action of cartels in seeking to maintain prices.   (25 marks)

Or

(e) With reference to the information provided and your own knowledge, evaluate the likely microeconomic and macroeconomic implications of a fall in world oil prices on the economies of Venezuela and the US.   (25 marks)

(e) While there is some potential overlap here with the microeconomic analysis of the effects on firms in question (b), if the same analysis is to be used again then it is important here to look at how those falls in costs will impact upon prices, profits and consumers. There is much that could be said on this question far beyond the scope of this book, such is the nature of a synoptic paper like this.

Selected responses:

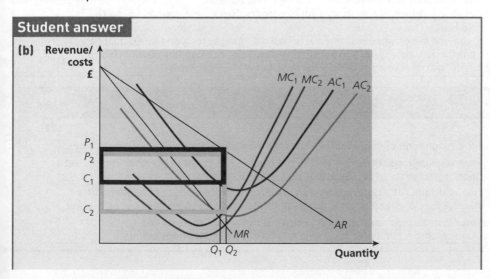

Student answer

(b)

(b) Falling oil prices mean that most firms will see a fall in variable and fixed costs. Oil is used as energy in production and for transport of raw materials and finished goods, as well as the costs of moving staff around the country. We would therefore expect a fall in AC and MC to AC_2 and MC_2 as shown in the diagram above. Profits would increase, as long as prices did not fall.

However, as costs fall we would expect more firms to enter the industry. So depending on how contestable the market is, we would expect prices also to fall, and profits might not increase as quickly.

ⓔ 8/8 marks awarded. KAA 6/6: good diagram with a clear rationale. Evaluation 2/2: one fair point made. It would be helpful to introduce the concept of elasticity, but there is enough here to earn both evaluation marks.

(e) The following table gives the format for an indicative mark scheme that you would expect to be used on your answer to question 2e. Note that the KAA (16) and evaluation (9) marks are given separately and will be awarded as discrete items.

Question number	Indicative content	Mark
2(e)	**Knowledge 4, Application 4, Analysis 8** Consideration must be given to both Venezuela and the US. Microeconomic implications: ■ oil producers: exports will fall in value because oil has very low *PED* ■ reduced producer surplus for exporting firms – many will reach shutdown point ■ increased consumer surplus in the US as oil-derived products become cheaper ■ shortages in shops: milk and toilet paper (Extract 1) are in short supply because of the difficulty in obtaining foreign currency ■ decreasing underlying value of currency and increasing costs in Venezuela (inflation of 63%) will decrease competitiveness of firms trying to export. Exporting firms may go out of business as importing firms are more competitive ■ workers in Venezuela may exit the labour market, e.g. through emigration. Macroeconomic implications: ■ worsening of the current account in Venezuela. Implications for foreign exchange reserves ■ weakening of the currency in Venezuela will further fuel inflation ■ falls in AD as X falls in Venezuela, with multiplier effects. Reverse is true in US as the value of imports falls ■ fiscal implications: the government in Venezuela has less money to spend on social projects ■ effect on Gini coefficient. Use of data to suggest widening of the gap between rich and poor in Venezuela and narrowing in the US (Lorenz curve may be used).	(16)

Question number	Indicative content	Mark
2(e)	**Evaluation 9** Consideration of the magnitude of the fall (30%) after a prolonged period of high export values. Short-run/long-run implications: the exporting firms might shut down in the short term, but this will mean much higher prices for US consumers in the long run. Effect on the US is uncertain. Although Venezuelan producers might go out of business, there are many other new sources of cheap oil emerging/substitutes such as shale gas now on market. Effects on inflation hard to know – not enough information, say, on the relaxed macroeconomic policy, or the ability for fiscal policy to be financed through bonds.	(9)

Knowledge check answers

1 A firm is a unit of production. It is the process by which factors of production are transformed into goods and services.

2 A firm is a production unit, whereas an industry is all the firms producing the same kind of output. For example, Nike is a firm producing sportswear in an industry including many big players, such as Adidas and Puma.

3 Profitability is a fairly unreliable measure of size, although many large firms do make a large percentage profit. Probably the best measure of the size of a firm is sales revenue as a percentage of the market, which closely correlates to the number of employees as a share of total workers in the industry.

4 Conglomerate integration, offering a wide scope of products such as offered by Virgin.

5 It is a 'corner' or a uniquely defined submarket which can be met by a small firm charging higher prices with a specific product, rather than a larger market that is more competitive which might enjoy lower costs.

6 Shareholders care most about profitability and the likelihood that share prices will rise (or fall if they are planning to sell). Managers often care deeply about the size of the firm as it correlates with the respect they feel they deserve, their chances of further promotions and the size of the bonus in many cases (where pay is linked to revenue).

7 It should get smaller. There will be a contraction along the long-run average cost ($LRAC$) curve and costs per unit then fall. This cost curve is explained on page 20.

8 Total revenue. This assumes that everyone pays the same price, or that the price is the average price.

9 $AR = P$: that is, the average revenue is the same as the price paid and so at any quantity it shows the demand.

10 When MC is below AC, it pulls AC down, and when MC is above AC, it pulls AC up. Only when $AC = MC$ is AC constant.

11 Falling. It means the firm is reducing output, which prevents the rise in costs that occurs when output rises.

12 If it produced any more then marginal profit would be less than zero, so total profit would fall.

13 $MR = 0$ is used by firms that do not need to take account of costs. If a firm has stock left over at the end of the day and it is going to pass its sell-by date, this is a rational policy, because the cost of the flowers is effectively zero and the firm might as well give them away. It is also rational for a firm's directors to revenue maximise if their pay is linked to sales revenue rather than profit.

14 High concentration means that a few firms dominate the market.

15 If price is not covering its AVC. In the short run, as long as it covers AVC, it will make a contribution to fixed costs. In the long run, the average variable cost is the same as average total costs (there are no fixed costs) so the rule still holds.

16 It cannot increase profit any further, either by increasing or by decreasing output, because either decreasing output ($MC < MR$) or increasing output ($MC > MR$) would lead to a fall in total profits. We are assuming that all firms aim to maximise profits and at $MC = MR$ marginal profit is zero, so no more profits can be made.

17 Because cutting prices tends to lead to a worse situation for all firms, as illustrated by a payoff matrix in game theory, or a discussion of price wars.

18 Both forms of collusion are usually found to be illegal, but tacit collusion in particular is very difficult to prove.

19 PED is relatively elastic.

20 The consumers with relatively price elastic demand benefit from lower prices and the firm benefits from higher profits. The loser appears to be the consumer who has no choice (lower PED) and has to pay the higher prices, such as commuters who need to use trains before 9.30 a.m. But you could argue that the higher profits might be beneficial for the people who pay the higher prices if they are invested back into the industry. There is plenty of scope for evaluation in this question.

21 Yes, any substantial lessening of competition by firms trying to limit opportunities for the seller may be judged to be illegal. For example, if the monopsonists forced suppliers to sell below cost price then the CMA could impose penalties.

22 A competitive market has many firms in the market, keeping prices low and output high. A contestable one has low barriers to entry or exit and behaves in response to the threat of competition, rather than the competition itself.

23 Demand in different economies is determined largely by incomes (as measured by GDP per head) but is also determined by leakages such as tax, imports or savings. This is a Theme 2 concept which can be used in a Paper 1 exam. Remember, Paper 3 at A-level is synoptic and can draw from material across the four themes. So you must get used to drawing from macro concepts at least from the start of your second year of the course.

24 Wages are just one of many factors that determine the supply of labour. Others include working conditions, the opportunity cost of leisure, migration, income tax, benefits, trade unions, government regulations and social trends.

25 An increase in productivity could shift demand for labour to the right if demand were based solely on MRP, or marginal revenue product (the amount the

worker adds to the firm through their labour). But because employers base their demand for labour on many things besides *MRP*, and can have monopsony (buying) power, the increase in productivity might simply feed through to increased profits for the employer rather than possible increases in wages as *MRP* rises.

26 It depends! Sometimes the rise in the NMW can increase the value of the productivity of workers and therefore increase the demand for labour. But otherwise, in Classical theory, a rise in NMW can, if above the labour market equilibrium, cause a surplus in the labour supply (unemployment). Keynesians would argue that the unemployment could in fact be caused by demand deficiency, in which case the rise in incomes could actually solve the unemployment problem. See Theme 2 for a full discussion of types of unemployment.

27 Competition authorities will allow mergers to go ahead if they believe there will not be a reduction in competition and the consumers will not be worse off. In most cases, especially now that economies operate in a globalised market with increased competition, mergers between firms will not result in a diminution of competition. That said, Ryanair had its attempt to buy Aer Lingus blocked three times by the EU and UK competition authorities as they felt it would reduce the choice consumers had on flights in and out of Ireland.

28 Privatisation is the sale of state-owned businesses into private ownership and was used heavily in the UK in the 1980s and early 1990s to raise revenue/stop losses for government and to place the businesses in the competitive market and therefore use the private sector to improve efficiency (the private sector is driven by the profit motive and so might be more willing to make efficiency cost cuts).

29 *X* represents the average efficiency savings that the firm is expected to be able to make and hence reflect in price cuts.

30 It is a penalty attached to a performance target.

Note: **Bold** page numbers indicate key term definitions.